Costa Rica Guide 2024

A Complete Pocket Guidebook to Exploring Beaches, Wildlife, Adventures and Outdoor Activities

ADELINE M. CREEL

All Rights Reserved!

No part of this book may be reproduced, stored in a retrieval system, or transmitted in any form or by any means, electronic, mechanical, photocopying, recording, or otherwise, without the prior written permission of the copyright owner. Copyright 2024, Adeline M. Creel.

TABLE OF CONTENT

Introduction 7
    Why Costa Rica? 8
    Travel Essentials 9
Planning Your Trip to Costa Rica 13
    The best time to visit 13
    Budgeting Your Trip 14
    Visa and Entry Requirements 16
    Health and Safety Tips 17
Transportation Options in Costa Rica 19
    Arrive in Costa Rica: Airports and Entry Points 19
    Transportation Options: From Buses to Car Rental 21
    Tips for Using Public Transportation 22
    Domestic flight and regional travel 23
Accommodation Options in Costa Rica 25
    How to Select the Right Lodging 25
    Eco-lodges & Sustainable Stays 27
    Best Hotels and Resorts for All Budgets 28
    Unique Accommodations 29
Culinary Delights: Exploring Costa Rican Cuisine 31
    Must-try dishes 32

Best Restaurants for All Tastes 33

Explore the Central Valley: San José and Surroundings. 36

San Jose: The Cultural Capital 36

Cultural attractions: 37

The surrounding regions 38

Natural Beauty and Adventure 40

Exploring the Caribbean Coast: Limón and Beyond. 42

Limón, the Cultural Melting Pot 42

Cultural highlights: 43

Sustainable Tourism and Community Engagement 46

Explore the Northern Plains: Arenal and La Fortuna. 48

Arenal Volcano 48

Arenal's thermal waters 49

La Fortuna 50

Adventure sports in the outdoors 52

Guanacaste: A Symphony of Beaches and National Parks. 54

Guanacaste's beaches. 54

Exploring Guanacaste's National Parks 56

Cultural Insights and Local Life 57

Southern Costa Rica & The Pacific Coast 59

Puntarenas: The Gateway to the Pacific. 59

Coastal Charms of Jacó and Manuel Antonio 60

4

- Osa Peninsula and Corcovado National Park 62
- Monteverde Cloud Forest: A Haven for Nature Lovers 65
  - Explore the Monteverde Cloud Forest Reserve. 66
  - Community and Culture in Monteverde 68
  - Visitor Info and Tips 69
- National Parks & Reserves in Costa Rica. 71
- Volcanoes and Hot Springs: Exploring Arenal, Poás, and Irazú 81
  - Arenal Volcano 81
  - Hot springs 82
  - Adventure Activities 83
  - Poás Volcano 83
  - Irazú Volcano 86
  - Benefits of Volcanic Hot Springs 88
- Costa Rica Beaches 90
  - Manuel Antonio 90
  - Uvita and Marino Ballena National Park 93
- Wildlife and Nature Tours 100
  - Bird Watching 100
- Activities and Tours in Costa Rica 110
  - Hiking and Trekking in Costa Rica 110
- Local Crafts and Shopping 122
  - Traditional crafts and artisanal souvenirs 122

Cultural experiences in Costa Rica. 133

    Costa Rican Culture 133

    Festivals and Events 136

    Experiencing Costa Rican culture firsthand 139

Travel Tips and Resources for Costa Rica 142

    Cultural Etiquette and Tips 145

    Practical Travel Tips: 149

Conclusion 153

Appendix 159

    Useful Apps 159

    Emergency Contacts 160

    Useful Phrases 160

    FAQs 161

    Travel Checklist 163

    Travel Itineraries 165

Introduction

Costa Rica, located between Nicaragua to the north and Panama to the south, is a dynamic treasure that welcomes visitors to discover its lush jungles, gorgeous beaches, and towering volcanoes. This little but mighty country has long been lauded for its conservation efforts and is a biodiversity hotspot, home to 5% of the world's species in its beautiful landscapes and calm oceans. Costa Rica's motto, "Pura Vida," which means 'pure life,' is more than simply a phrase; it embodies the Costa Rican culture's excitement and love for life.

When you step foot in this wonderful country, you are not just a visitor, but a participant in a profound ecological and cultural experience. The kindness of the locals complements the country's tropical atmosphere, making each interaction unforgettable. Whether it's your first visit or you're returning to rediscover its delights, Costa Rica has an unending list of activities that may elevate the ordinary to the spectacular.

Costa Rica's soul is tangible, from the vibrant streets of San José to the serene beaches of the Caribbean coast. Each location offers a unique tapestry of activities, scenery, and weather, encouraging visitors to enjoy both adventure and relaxation. In this context, the natural environment is critical to daily living. As a guest, you'll quickly realize that sustainability is more than just a phrase; it's woven into the fabric of everything from hotel operations to tour activities, reflecting the country's pioneering approach to environmental preservation.

Why Costa Rica?

Travelers are drawn to Costa Rica for a variety of compelling reasons. Adventurers find peace in adrenaline-pumping activities such as whitewater rafting, zip-lining through cloud forests, and surfing on both the Pacific and Atlantic beaches. Those seeking quiet will find it while roaming through tropical botanical gardens, relaxing at hot springs, or performing yoga on a remote beach at sunset.

Additionally, Costa Rica's biodiversity is unrivaled. Imagine seeing a sloth in its native habitat, watching a sea turtle nesting, or hearing the haunting sounds of howler monkeys at dawn. The prospects for wildlife interactions here are as diverse as the ecosystems themselves, providing remarkable moments of connection to nature.

Travel Essentials

Planning a vacation to Costa Rica is an exciting endeavor, but it takes careful planning to ensure a smooth and pleasurable journey. Here are some important suggestions and standards to consider before beginning on your Costa Rica journey.

When to Visit: Timing is essential when arranging a trip to Costa Rica. The country has two main seasons: the dry season (December to April) and the rainy season (May to November). Each season provides distinct advantages. The dry season, with its sunny, clear days, is great for exploring coastal areas and enjoying sunbathing or water sports. In contrast, the rainy season brings out the lushness of the rainforests, waterfalls in full splendor, and fewer visitors, allowing for a more intimate experience with nature.

Health & Safety: Costa Rica is generally safe for visitors, with a well-established tourist infrastructure and pleasant natives eager to assist. However, it is prudent to take conventional safety precautions such as avoiding lonely regions at night, only using licensed taxis, and remaining educated about local conditions.

Health-wise, make sure you're up to date on basic vaccines, and it's best to see a travel health clinic before your trip, especially if you want to visit isolated places. Tap water is safe to drink in the majority of the country, but bottled water is recommended for rural places.

Local Currency and Payment: The local currency is the Costa Rican Colón (CRC), but US dollars are often accepted in tourist regions. It's a good idea to carry some local cash for little transactions because not all sellers take credit cards, especially in less tourist areas. ATMs are widely available in major cities and towns, however, it's best to notify your bank of your travel plans to avoid any card complications while abroad.

Language & Communication: Spanish is the official language of Costa Rica. English is frequently spoken in popular tourist destinations, but learning a few basic Spanish words can help you communicate with locals and enrich your experience. Costa Ricans, often known as Ticos, are recognized for their friendliness and hospitality, frequently going out of their way to help visitors.

Sustainable Travel Practices: Costa Rica, a conservation leader, encourages visitors to practice responsible tourism. This involves protecting wildlife and natural ecosystems, selecting eco-friendly excursions and accommodations, and limiting plastic use. Traveling with respect helps to preserve the natural splendor that makes Costa Rica a nature lover's paradise.

Traveling to Costa Rica is more than just a vacation; it's a dynamic, instructive, and transforming experience with something for everyone. Whether you're admiring volcanic vistas, relaxing on sun-kissed beaches, or exploring lush jungles, Costa Rica promises an amazing trip steeped in the essence of Pura Vida.

Planning Your Trip to Costa Rica

Traveling to Costa Rica provides an amazing combination of excitement and relaxation. However, appropriate preparation is essential for a successful encounter. Every part of your travel planning is critical, from selecting the best time to visit to budgeting and knowing visa procedures. Here's a complete tutorial to help you explore these critical components.

The best time to visit

When to visit Costa Rica is mostly determined by your weather choices, type of activity, and tolerance for crowds. The country's climate is generally tropical all year, yet it can be separated into two seasons: dry and wet (or green).

Dry Season (December to April): Known locally as Verano (summer), these months are distinguished by bright days and clear skies, making them ideal for beach activities, hiking, and animal watching. This is peak tourist season, so while the weather is ideal, expect higher pricing and more congested attractions.

Rainy Season (May to November): Also known as invierno (winter), this season brings regular rain showers, usually in the afternoon, resulting in lush, bright landscapes and a dramatic increase in river levels, suitable for rafting. The rainy season has the advantage of lower rates and fewer tourists, resulting in more intimate contact with nature and local culture.

The transitional months, notably May and November, can provide a sweet spot with fewer tourists and temperate weather, making them worthwhile for anyone seeking a combination of quiet and accessibility.

Budgeting Your Trip

Costa Rica can cater to a variety of budgets, from backpackers to luxury travelers. Here's how to plan your finances:

Accommodation: Accommodation options range from low-cost hostels (about $15 per night) to luxury resorts or eco-lodges (up to $250 per night). Mid-range hotels are typically priced between $50 and $150 per night.

Food: Local eateries, known as sodas, serve traditional Costa Rican cuisine for $3-$7 each meal. Dining at mid-range restaurants often costs between $10 and $25 per person, whereas high-end restaurants may charge $30 or more per meal.

Transportation: Public buses are the most affordable way to travel around the country, with fares ranging from $1 to $10 depending on distance. Renting a car provides additional freedom, but expect to pay between $30 and $100 per day. Domestic flights to isolated places, such as the Osa Peninsula, can cost between $50 and $150 one way.

Activities: National parks generally charge entry fees ranging from $10 to $20. Guided tours, such as animal watching or adventure sports, can cost anywhere from $35 to more than $100, depending on the activity and duration.

Miscellaneous: Always reserve a portion of your money for unforeseen expenses, souvenirs, and tips for guides and service personnel.

Visa and Entry Requirements

For the majority of travelers, entering Costa Rica is uncomplicated. Visitors from the United States, Canada, and most European nations do not require a visa for visits of up to 90 days. Requirements include:

- A valid passport with at least six months remaining before it expires.
- Proof of continued or return travel.
- Sufficient finances for the duration of the stay (usually about $100 each week).

Travelers from other countries may require a visa, so contact the nearest Costa Rican embassy or consulate before planning your trip.

Health and Safety Tips

While Costa Rica is one of the safest countries for tourists in Latin America, following some measures will help you have a trouble-free vacation.

Health: No particular immunizations are required for entrance, but vaccines for Hepatitis A and Typhoid are advised because of their frequency in warmer climes. Mosquitoes can transmit diseases such as Zika, Dengue, and Chikungunya, thus protection is critical.

Safety: Use common sense, as you would in any tourist site. Avoid carrying significant quantities of cash, keep valuables locked, and stay in well-trafficked locations, especially at night. Tap water is generally safe to drink in Costa Rica, but bottled water is recommended in more rural regions.

Sustainable Travel Tips

Costa Rica is a leader in sustainable tourism. To support their conservation efforts, consider the following:

Choose Sustainable Operators: Look for tours and accommodations with sustainable certifications, such as the Certification for Sustainable Tourism (CST).

Respect Wildlife: Keep a safe distance from animals to avoid stress and injury. Never feed wildlife or try to get their attention for photographs.

Reduce Plastic Waste: Bring reusable water bottles, bags, and straws to reduce your plastic footprint.

Support Local Communities: Work with local guides and buy local items to boost the local economy and lower the carbon footprint involved with importing things.

You can expect an enriching and delightful visit to Costa Rica if you properly plan your trip, stick to your budget, respect local laws and customs, and engage in sustainable behaviors. This magnificent country offers more than simply a vacation; it allows you to connect with nature, experience authentic culture, and make experiences that will last a lifetime.

Transportation Options in Costa Rica

Costa Rica, a jewel tucked in the heart of Central America, is a location that provides not only magnificent landscapes but also a well-connected network of transportation alternatives for all types of travelers. Understanding the logistics of getting there and about is critical to a smooth travel experience, from the minute you land to your daily adventures.

Arrive in Costa Rica: Airports and Entry Points

Costa Rica's main international airports are Juan Santamaría International Airport (SJO) in Alajuela, near San José, and Daniel Oduber Quirós International Airport (LIR) in Liberia.

Juan Santamaría International Airport (SJO) is the larger and busier of the two major airports, located near the capital city of San José. It acts as a hub for arriving flights from North America, Europe, and other parts of Latin America. The airport is well-equipped with vehicle rental companies, dependable taxi services, and direct bus lines that connect visitors to San José and other key cities throughout the country.

Daniel Oduber Quirós International Airport (LIR) is located in Liberia, Guanacaste's capital, and serves as a gateway to Costa Rica's spectacular Pacific Coast beaches and northern regions. It has gained in popularity, particularly among travelers seeking to enjoy the natural splendor of the country's western region without having to pass through San José.

For travelers from neighboring countries, smaller entry ports like Tobias Bolaños Airport in San José and Limón International Airport on the Caribbean side provide regional connectivity.

Transportation Options: From Buses to Car Rental

Costa Rica can be navigated via a variety of modes of transportation, each with its distinct balance of convenience, expense, and excitement.

Buses: The most cost-effective way to travel around Costa Rica is by bus. The country has a vast network of public buses that connects almost every town and city. These buses range from opulent coaches for long-distance routes to simple but practical vehicles for shorter excursions. Major bus terminals in San José, such as Terminal 7-10, serve as main hubs for lines that connect the entire country.

Car Rentals: Car rentals offer flexibility and are great for individuals who want to explore Costa Rica at their leisure. Several reputable rental firms have locations in both major airports and large cities. While a 4x4 is ideal for rural areas, especially during the rainy season, smaller cars are adequate for well-trafficked routes in and around towns. Before you go on your travel, make sure to verify the road conditions and your insurance coverage.

Taxis and ridesharing: Taxis are a safe and convenient choice, especially in urban areas. They can be hailed on the street or booked through a variety of taxi services. Ridesharing apps, such as Uber, are accessible in major cities and can be an affordable and convenient alternative.

Shared Vans & Shuttles: For individuals searching for a compromise between the cost of buses and the convenience of cabs, shared shuttle services are a viable option. These shuttles offer pre-booked, direct service to popular tourist locations and frequently include hotel pickups and drop-offs.

Tips for Using Public Transportation

Plan ahead of time: Check timetables and routes, especially if you're taking public transportation. While Costa Rica's bus network is substantial, the frequency varies drastically depending on the location.

22

Carry Small Change: When paying bus or taxi fares, it's a good idea to have small denominations of the local currency on hand, as drivers may not always have change for larger bills.

Confirm the Price: Before boarding a cab, ask if the fare is metered or set. If the fee is established, agree on it before you start your travel to avoid misunderstandings.

Safety First: Always keep your possessions secure and be aware of your surroundings, especially on public transit and at busy terminals.

Domestic flight and regional travel

For individuals who are short on time or want to avoid long road trips, domestic flights can be a good option. Several local airlines connect San José with popular tourist destinations such as Quepos, Tamarindo, Tortuguero, and the Osa Peninsula. These flights are often short, lasting 30 to 60 minutes, and offer breathtaking aerial views of Costa Rica's various landscapes.

Booking in Advance: To get the best fares and ensure availability, especially during peak seasons, book domestic flights well in advance.

Luggage Restrictions: Be aware of luggage restrictions on smaller planes. Weight limits can be stringent, and packing light is generally more cost-effective.

Navigating Costa Rica's diverse range of transport alternatives is part of the adventure that this dynamic country provides. Whether you select land or air travel, each offers a distinct view of Costa Rica's diverse ecosystems, cultures, and experiences.

Accommodation Options in Costa Rica.

Costa Rica, with its rich biodiversity and breathtaking scenery, provides a wide range of lodging options to suit any traveler's preferences and budget. From eco-lodges buried in the middle of the jungle to opulent beachside resorts and one-of-a-kind treehouses, the options are as varied as the country's nature. This guide will assist you in selecting the ideal hotel that not only meets your preferences but also enriches your trip experience in this lovely country.

How to Select the Right Lodging

Choosing where to stay in Costa Rica can have a huge impact on your overall experience. Here are a few considerations to consider while choosing your accommodation:

Location: Choose your preferred setting—be it the beach, mountains, city, or distant jungle. Each location provides a unique experience and may affect access to attractions and activities.

Budget: Determine how much you are willing to spend each night. Costa Rica's housing options range from low-cost hostels to mid-range hotels and luxury resorts.

Amenities: Consider what amenities you value, such as free Wi-Fi, air conditioning, complimentary breakfast, or a swimming pool.

Travel Style: Whether you seek luxury, adventure, or a cultural experience, the sort of accommodation you select might influence your travel style. Eco-lodges, for example, are ideal for nature enthusiasts and adventurers, but boutique hotels may appeal to those looking for a cultural immersion experience.

Reviews: Always read recent reviews from other travelers. They can provide information about the quality of service, cleanliness, and actual experiences that photographs and descriptions do not necessarily represent.

Eco-lodges & Sustainable Stays

Costa Rica is a leader in ecotourism and sustainability, with some of the world's top eco-lodges. These lodgings are intended to minimize environmental effects while providing guests with an authentic natural experience. Here are the major characteristics and some top recommendations.

Integration with Nature: Eco-lodges are frequently built in or near nature reserves using sustainable materials that mix in with the surroundings.

Sustainability Practices: These lodges follow ideas such as water conservation, solar energy, and garbage recycling. They frequently provide organic, locally sourced meals and participate in community enrichment initiatives.

Recommended eco-lodges:

Lapa Rios Lodge: Lapa Rios Lodge on the Osa Peninsula is well-known for its conservation and community-benefit initiatives.

Finca Rosa Blanca Coffee Plantation Resort: combines luxury and environmental sensitivity, with its organic coffee plantation and exquisite biodiversity.

Staying at an eco-lodge allows you to not only see Costa Rica's animals up close but also helps conservation efforts and local people.

Best Hotels and Resorts for All Budgets

Budget-Friendly Hotels

Hotel La Fortuna: Located near the Arenal Volcano, it provides basic amenities and comfort at an affordable price, making it perfect for backpackers and budget travelers.

Mid-range Hotels:

El Establo Mountain Hotel: in Monteverde offers great value with comfortable rooms, stunning views, and easy access to cloud forest areas.

Luxury resorts:

The Springs Resort and Spa: The Springs Resort and Spa in Arenal offers hot springs, an on-site wildlife sanctuary, and magnificent amenities for a unique experience.

Unique Accommodations

For those looking for a unique experience, Costa Rica has a variety of unorthodox lodging options, such as treehouses and bungalows that allow you to live in nature.

Treehouse accommodations:

Tree House Lodge: in Punta Uva offers both adventure and comfort. Located on the Caribbean coast, it's ideal for people who want to wake up to the sounds of waves and birds.

Finca Bellavista Treehouse Community: provides a network of sustainable treehouses in the South Pacific region that can only be accessed via zip-line or hiking trails.

Beachfront bungalows:

Ylang Ylang Beach Resort: in Montezuma offers beachfront bungalows with solitude and spectacular ocean views, ideal for honeymoons or romantic holidays.

Each of these lodgings offers a unique perspective on life in Costa Rica, allowing you to select the style that best suits your travel narrative while immersing yourself in the region's natural beauty and culture.

By taking these aspects and possibilities into account, you may locate the ideal place to stay that not only matches your needs but also improves your Costa Rica travel experience. Whether you choose the rustic appeal of an eco-lodge, the opulence of a beachside resort, or the novelty of a treehouse, your lodging option will be an important part of your trip in this dynamic country.

Culinary Delights: Exploring Costa Rican Cuisine

Costa Rica, a destination known not just for its breathtaking vistas but also for its thriving culinary scene, provides a flavor palette as diverse as its ecosystems. The country's food is a delectable blend of textures and flavors, founded in its agricultural background and enriched by its tropical bounty. This guide will take you through the must-try dishes and beverages, as well as recommendations for the top dining experiences in the country.

Costa Rican cuisine is noted for its emphasis on freshness and simplicity, using locally sourced ingredients including corn, beans, rice, plantains, and a variety of tropical fruits and vegetables. The culinary experience here is more than just food; it is a celebration of community and family, as evidenced by the traditional feasts enjoyed throughout the country.

Must-try dishes

Gallo Pinto: is a tasty combination of rice and black beans sautéed with onions, bell peppers, and seasonings that is frequently eaten as a morning dish. It is frequently served with eggs, plantains, and a thick, sour salsa known as Salsa Lizano.

Casado: A casado is the standard Costa Rican lunch meal, consisting of rice, beans, salad, a choice of protein (such as fish, chicken, hog, or cattle), and fried plantains. This dish is a full and balanced supper that highlights the simplicity and freshness of locally sourced ingredients.

Ceviche: Costa Rican ceviche is a must-try for seafood enthusiasts. Fresh fish is marinated in lime juice, onions, cilantro, and peppers. This meal is pleasantly tart and is frequently served with crunchy corn tortillas.

Arroz con leche: is a creamy rice pudding cooked with cinnamon and sugar that is frequently served with raisins or a dusting of fresh nutmeg.

Beverages:

Coffee: As one of the world's largest coffee exporters, Costa Rican coffee is a must-try. The rich volcanic soil provides the coffee with a distinct and powerful flavor. Visit a local café or join a coffee plantation tour to sample some of the greatest brews.

Fresco de Frutas: is a popular non-alcoholic beverage produced by blending or squeezing fruit with water or milk and sweetened to taste. It's refreshing and goes wonderfully with Costa Rica's tropical climate.

Guaro: Guaro, a sugarcane liquor, is a popular local alcohol in Costa Rica. It is commonly consumed as a shot or incorporated into drinks such as the 'guaro sour'.

Best Restaurants for All Tastes

Whether you want a lavish dining experience or a simple yet tasty dinner, Costa Rica has restaurants to suit every taste and budget.

Fine dining:

Grano de Oro Restaurant, San José: Located in the Hotel Grano de Oro, this restaurant serves a refined menu combining Costa Rican and European cuisines prepared with the freshest local products.

Restaurante 1687, Monteverde: Named after the year coffee was first introduced to Costa Rica, this farm-to-table establishment serves cuisine made from local ingredients and complemented with great local wines.

Casual and Mid-Range Eats:

Soda Tapia, San José: A popular place among locals, Soda Tapia serves traditional Costa Rican cuisine in a relaxed atmosphere. It's ideal for those wishing to enjoy real local cuisine without breaking the bank.

Lanterna Italian Steakhouse, La Fortuna: For those who enjoy Italian cuisine, this steakhouse offers superb steaks and pasta dishes with a Costa Rican touch.

Unique dining experiences:

El Avion, Manuel Antonio: El Avion offers a meal with a view and a one-of-a-kind atmosphere inside a converted airplane. The restaurant has amazing ocean views and provides a combination of Costa Rican and foreign cuisine.

Tree House Restaurant and Café, Monteverde: This restaurant, built around a massive ficus tree, provides an unforgettable dining experience under the canopy of Monteverde's cloud forest. Dine amid nature and enjoy the ambiance and good local coffee.

Whether you're indulging in a sumptuous meal, enjoying the simplicity of a casado, or drinking freshly brewed coffee, Costa Rica's culinary experiences are sure to be as enriching as its surroundings. Each meal provides insight into the country's culture and traditions, making dining an essential element of the Costa Rican tourist experience.

Explore the Central Valley: San José and Surroundings.

Costa Rica's Central Valley is not just the country's geographic heart, but also its cultural and political center. This region, which includes the capital city of San José as well as its surrounding cities and rural areas, provides an appealing combination of urban experiences and natural beauty. From lively markets and museums to calm coffee farms and volcanic scenery, the Central Valley offers a glimpse into Costa Rican culture that is rich in history and variety.

San Jose: The Cultural Capital

San José is Costa Rica's dynamic core, full of energy and cultural heritage. Travelers eager to get to the ocean or the cloud woods frequently reject the city, but those who stay gain a comprehensive picture of Costa Rica's past and present.

Cultural attractions:

The National Theatre of Costa Rica: which opened in 1897, is a testimony to the country's rich artistic tradition. The theatre has a regular program of performances ranging from opera to symphony concerts, and its luxurious interior is decorated with costly furnishings and exquisite murals.

The Museum of Costa Rican Art: is housed in a structure that was originally the city's major airport and displays work by renowned Costa Rican artists from the mid-19th century to the present. The park that surrounds the museum is popular with both locals and visitors.

The Central Market (Mercado Central): founded in 1880, is a bustling tangle of over 200 shops, stalls, and tiny restaurants (sodas). It provides a real local experience, allowing you to try traditional meals, buy local handicrafts, and see daily life in the bustling marketplace.

Food & Dining:

San José is a gastronomic melting pot, reflecting the city's decades-long immigration history. The eating scene includes everything from traditional Costa Rican dishes served in local cafes to new fusion cuisine in elite restaurants. Coffee culture is also prevalent here, with many cafes serving locally sourced beans and employing artisanal brewing methods.

The surrounding regions

Beyond San José's urban scene, the Central Valley boasts a range of natural attractions and quieter communities, each with its distinct appeal.

Heredia: City of Flowers: Heredia, located just north of San José, is renowned as the "City of Flowers" for its beautiful scenery and abundance of flowers. The city itself has a relaxing vibe, complete with a gorgeous center park and old buildings. Visitors can visit nearby coffee estates for guided tours and tastings, which provide insights into the entire coffee-making process from bean to cup.

Alajuela: Gateway to Volcanoes: Travelers arriving or departing from Juan Santamaría International Airport frequently make their first or last stop in Alajuela. However, it's worth a visit in and of itself because of its proximity to two of Costa Rica's most famous volcanoes:

Poás Volcano: Poás is one of the country's most active volcanoes, and its major crater has an outstanding sulfuric lake. The adjacent national park has well-marked paths and beautiful scenery.

Arenal Volcano: Arenal, located further north but still accessible from Alajuela, is one of Costa Rica's most iconic and active volcanoes. The Arenal area is a popular destination for adventure tourism, with trekking, hot springs, and water sports available at Lake Arenal.

Cartago, Costa Rica's Old Capital: Cartago, located east of San José, served as Costa Rica's capital until

1823. This city is rich in history, with several notable colonial remains and religious structures, including the Basilica of Our Lady of the Angels, which is a popular pilgrimage site for Costa Ricans. The lush Orosi Valley nearby provides gorgeous drives and is a paradise for people interested in rural tourism and local crafts.

Natural Beauty and Adventure

The entire Central Valley is an ideal destination for outdoor enthusiasts. The region's rich volcanic soil creates a tapestry of agricultural farms, woodlands, and plantations. Hiking, bird viewing, and cycling are popular activities that allow tourists to experience the valley's natural splendor.

Visiting the Central Valley gives you a better perspective of Costa Rica than just its beaches and biodiverse rainforests. This region combines cultural richness, historical significance, and natural beauty, making it a must-see for any complete Costa Rica visit. Whether you're exploring the busy streets of San José, enjoying the calm beauty of Heredia, or adventuring near the volcanoes of Alajuela, the Central Valley welcomes everyone who wants to get deeper into the heart of Costa Rica.

Exploring the Caribbean Coast: Limón and Beyond.

The Caribbean Coast of Costa Rica, which stretches from the northern border with Nicaragua to the southern extremities near Panama, has a unique vibe when contrasted to the Pacific side. This region, with its rich Afro-Caribbean tradition, lush rainforests, and laid-back coastal communities, offers a distinct blend of natural beauty, culture, and history. Limón, the busy core of this coastline, is the ideal starting place for discovering the area's many attractions.

Limón, the Cultural Melting Pot

Limón is more than just a city; it's a rich cultural tapestry. Limón, which has been influenced by several cultures, including Afro-Caribbean, Bribri Indigenous, and Latino, has a fascinating history and a vibrant cultural scene. The annual funfair, one of Costa Rica's most anticipated events, features colorful parades, music, and dancing that reflect the diverse community.

Cultural highlights:

Carnival of Limón: The Limón Carnival, held in October, fills the streets with vivid costumes, calypso music, and dance acts that celebrate the city's ethnic background.

Afro-Caribbean Cuisine: Limón's food scene is a wonderful example of its ethnic variety. Traditional foods include coconut milk-cooked rice and beans, Rondon (a savory seafood stew), and patty (a spicy beef pastry).

Museo Etnohistórico de Limón: The Museo Etnohistórico de Limón provides insights into the city's complex cultural tapestry by describing the history of its Indigenous and Afro-Caribbean communities.

Beyond Limón: Natural Wonders & Serene Beaches

Traveling south from Limón, the coastline is lined with peaceful communities and gorgeous nature reserves. Each destination has its distinct appeal and variety of activities for nature lovers, beachgoers, and adventurers.

Tortuguero National Park: Tortuguero National Park, accessible only by boat or light plane, is known as the "Amazon of Costa Rica." It is one of the best areas in the country to see tropical rainforest biodiversity. It is also known for its turtle nesting beaches, where visitors may watch sea turtles deposit their eggs throughout the nesting season.

Wildlife Watching: The park's network of rivers and canals provides a good opportunity for guided boat rides, allowing you to see sloths, howler monkeys, river otters, and a variety of bird species.

Turtle Nesting Tours: Depending on the time of year, night tours offer a unique opportunity to observe green turtles (from July to October) and leatherback turtles (from February to April) nest.

Cahuita National Park, Puerto Viejo: Cahuita National Park and the hamlet of Puerto Viejo, located further down the coast, are recognized for their relaxed attitude, magnificent beaches, and outstanding surfing areas. Puerto Viejo's bustling nightlife and unique food scene make it especially popular with younger travelers and surfers.

Snorkeling and Diving: Cahuita National Park has some of the best snorkeling and diving in Costa Rica, with its protected coral reefs home to a diversity of marine species.

Cultural Experience: Puerto Viejo has a strong Rastafarian influence, as evidenced by its music culture and citizens' easygoing lifestyles.

Gandoca-Manzanillo Wildlife Refuge: This less-traveled sanctuary is ideal for animal enthusiasts and those seeking tranquility. The location includes quiet beaches, mangroves, and a lowland tropical rainforest.

Hiking and Bird Watching: Explore the refuge's pathways to learn about its different ecosystems and see some of the region's unique bird species.

Relax on Secluded Beaches: The beaches of Manzanillo are ideal for anyone wishing to escape the more busy areas further north.

Sustainable Tourism and Community Engagement

Costa Rica's Caribbean Coast is not just a zone of breathtaking natural beauty, but it is also a site where sustainable tourism practices are making substantial progress. Many of the eco-lodges and tour companies here are actively involved in wildlife conservation and community development initiatives. Visitors can participate with local communities by taking cultural tours, volunteering, and supporting local craftsmen and businesses.

Costa Rica's Caribbean coast combines cultural richness, environmental diversity, and adventure. From Limón's cultural celebrations to the natural splendor of its national parks and the tranquil beauty of its beaches, this region offers a journey of discovery and delight. Whether you want to immerse yourself in Afro-Caribbean culture, go on an eco-adventure in the jungle, or simply relax by the shore, the Caribbean Coast will enchant and inspire everyone who visits.

Explore the Northern Plains: Arenal and La Fortuna.

The Arenal region, located in Costa Rica's Northern Plains, is a natural wonderland full of adventure and beauty. This location, dominated by the majestic silhouette of Arenal Volcano, provides a mix of adrenaline activities, relaxing hot springs, and diverse wildlife. La Fortuna, a lovely village located just a few kilometers from the volcano, serves as the region's entrance, providing a comfortable base for adventurers and nature enthusiasts. This book looks into the key experiences and sights that make Arenal and La Fortuna a must-see destinations in Costa Rica.

Arenal Volcano

The Arenal Volcano, which stands at 1,657 meters, is both a breathtaking icon and the focal point of the region's tourism operations. The volcano, which was once very active, has been dormant since 2010, but it continues to attract visitors from all around the world.

Volcano Viewing: The best views of Arenal may be seen at numerous locations around La Fortuna. The Arenal Observatory Lodge provides one of the most outstanding vantage sites, with trails that allow for closer views in safe conditions.

Hiking Opportunities: Numerous paths surround the volcano, each suited to a different degree of fitness. These routes offer not only volcanic landscapes but also passages through rainforests and past waterfalls where visitors can study the local flora and fauna in their natural habitat.

Arenal's thermal waters

Arenal is well-known for its natural hot springs, which are generated by geothermal activity beneath the volcano. These springs are not only relaxing, but they also provide health benefits due to their mineral-rich qualities.

Tabacón Thermal Resort & Spa: Tabacón, one of the area's first and most magnificent hot springs resorts, features a network of naturally running thermal rivers nestled within lush tropical gardens, creating an idyllic relaxing atmosphere.

Baldi Hot Springs: Known for having the most thermal pools, Baldi offers a pleasant and family-friendly ambiance with amenities for both leisure and amusement, such as waterslides and swim-up bars.

La Fortuna

La Fortuna is more than just the nearest town to Arenal Volcano; it is a thriving community full of culture and hospitality. The town has a variety of dining and lodging alternatives, appealing to both backpackers and luxury travelers.

Local Cuisine: Dining in La Fortuna provides an opportunity to sample traditional Costa Rican meals such as "casado" or "ceviche," which are served in the town's numerous sodas (small, informal restaurants).

For a more expensive dining experience, some gourmet restaurants provide stunning views of the Arenal Volcano to complement their fine menus.

Cultural Experiences: The town's central park is a favorite gathering place for both locals and tourists, and it frequently hosts cultural events and festivals that highlight local music, dancing, and crafts.

Ecotourism and Conservation Efforts

Arenal and La Fortuna are not just tourist destinations, but also important sites for environmental conservation. The region's great biodiversity is preserved under several reserves and national parks, all of which emphasize sustainable tourist practices.

Arenal Volcano National Park protects ecosystems ranging from rainforest to cloud forest, offering secure habitats for sloths, jaguars, and a variety of bird species. Guided tours of the park provide information about the area's ecological importance and attempts to preserve it.

Mistico Arenal Hanging Bridges Park: This park features a series of suspension bridges that provide a unique view of the rainforest canopy. It is intended to fit with the natural environment, reducing human disturbance while providing for great wildlife watching.

Adventure sports in the outdoors

Arenal and La Fortuna provide a variety of adventure activities set against the backdrop of the region's breathtaking surroundings.

White-Water Rafting: The rivers of La Fortuna, particularly the Toro and Balsa, provide thrilling rafting adventures for all ability levels.

Zip-Lining: Several operators provide zip-lining experiences that take you above the treetops and provide stunning views of the area's natural splendor.

Canyoning and Waterfall Rappelling: These activities combine hiking, climbing, and rappelling, providing an exciting opportunity to explore the rainforest's less accessible areas.

The Arenal and La Fortuna region exemplifies Costa Rica's essence: a land of natural beauty and adventure. Whether relaxing in hot springs, hiking rainforest paths, or experiencing the warmth of local friendliness, travelers to this area have an amazing experience that embodies the essence of Pura Vida, Costa Rica's pure life.

Guanacaste: A Symphony of Beaches and National Parks.

Guanacaste, located in northwestern Costa Rica, is known for its stunning coastline, expansive national parks, and strong cultural history. This area, often known as the "Gold Coast," is home to some of Central America's most stunning beaches, as well as a rich array of ecosystems that provide habitat for a wide range of wildlife.

Whether you're sunbathing on sun-kissed beaches, exploring green forests, or experiencing local traditions, Guanacaste has a diverse range of activities that appeal to nature lovers, adventurers, and cultural aficionados.

Guanacaste's beaches.

Guanacaste's coastline runs for 200 kilometers and boasts a gorgeous collection of beaches that are as diverse as they are picturesque. From bustling beach cities to isolated bays, each beach has its distinct appeal and variety of activities.

Playa Conchal: Playa Conchal is widely recognized as one of Costa Rica's most beautiful beaches, because of its sparkling white shells and crystal-clear water. Its turquoise waters and serene atmosphere make it ideal for leisure and recreation, as well as snorkelling and water sports.

Tamarindo: Tamarindo is the vibrant and lively center of Guanacaste surf culture. This beach is known not only for its superb surf breaks but also for its vibrant nightlife and gastronomic scene. Tamarindo is also a convenient starting point for seeing other local sights, making it a popular tourist destination.

Playa Flamingo: is a tropical paradise, complete with immaculate white sand and lovely blue waters. It is also a top destination for deep-sea fishing, with the potential to catch marlin, sailfish, and tuna.

Samara: A hidden gem away from the more tourist-heavy destinations, Samara provides a delightful blend of local culture and natural beauty. Samara's coral reef protects its bay, making it an ideal destination for families and anyone seeking calmer waters for swimming and snorkeling.

Exploring Guanacaste's National Parks

Guanacaste is known for more than only its stunning beaches; it also has huge, protected wilderness regions that are important for environmental conservation and offer exhilarating adventures.

Rincón de la Vieja National Park: Renowned for its active volcano, hot springs, and rich wildlife, Rincón de la Vieja is a paradise for travelers. The park's numerous trails lead to breathtaking waterfalls, boiling mud pots, and fumaroles, allowing visitors to witness nature's power firsthand.

Santa Rosa National Park: As one of Costa Rica's oldest and most important national parks, Santa Rosa is an important place for both ecological preservation and historical value. It protects some of the world's last remaining tropical dry forests and contains the historic Battle of Santa Rosa site.

Palo Verde National Park: is a birdwatcher's dream, with both dry forest and marsh environments. During the rainy season, the park's floodplains serve as temporary homes for hundreds of bird species, including the endangered jabiru stork.

Marino Las Baulas National Park: is one of the most important nesting grounds for the leatherback turtle, an endangered species. Night tours allow tourists to observe the wonderful process of giant turtles laying eggs in the moonlight.

Cultural Insights and Local Life

Guanacaste's culture is heavily founded in agricultural traditions, particularly cattle ranching, which is honored at a variety of local festivals that include music, dance, and bull riding. The "sabanero" cowboy culture is a proud symbol of Guanacaste's heritage, and it can be seen in cities like Santa Cruz, also known as the "National Folklore City."

Local Festivals: The yearly Fiestas Civicas include traditional rodeos, horse parades (topes), and marimba music, providing a colorful glimpse into Guanacaste's cultural life.

Culinary Delights: Guanacaste's cuisine reflects its agricultural background, with meals featuring corn, beans, and a variety of fresh fish. "Casado" is a classic cuisine that consists of rice, beans, salad, plantain, and a choice of meat or fish.

Artisanal Crafts: The region is well-known for its pottery and leatherwork. The small community of Guaitil, for example, is well-known for its traditional Chorotega pottery crafted with ancient indigenous traditions.

Guanacaste has a rich tapestry of activities that go far beyond its beaches. Its national parks provide adventures in wild settings, while its people welcome visitors with vibrant cultural traditions. Whether you want to relax on a tranquil beach, explore volcanic wonders, or participate in traditional celebrations, Guanacaste is the ideal setting for a wonderful Costa Rican vacation.

Southern Costa Rica & The Pacific Coast

Southern Costa Rica, which stretches from the lively coastal city of Puntarenas to the distant wilds of Corcovado, provides a striking contrast between accessible attractions and unspoiled natural beauty. This region offers a mix of breathtaking scenery, from pristine beaches and picturesque coastal villages to some of the world's most biodiverse rainforests. Each site on the Pacific Coast offers distinct options for adventure, leisure, and cultural immersion, making it a must-see for visitors looking to see Costa Rica's unspoiled side.

Puntarenas: The Gateway to the Pacific.

Puntarenas, formerly a bustling port and fishing city, now serves as a gateway to Costa Rica's southern Pacific coast. This city, with its long, narrow peninsula protruding into the Gulf of Nicoya, serves as a jumping-off place for people who want to explore the surrounding area.

Attractions in Puntarenas:

Marine Park: Visitors may learn about marine conservation and witness numerous marine species up close.

Historical Nautical Museum: Here, tourists may learn about Costa Rica's rich nautical history and the important role Puntarenas has played.

Local Cuisine: Puntarenas is well-known for its seafood, particularly "ceviche," a dish made from fresh fish cured in citrus juices and served with onions, cilantro, and chili peppers.

Travelers frequently take boats from Puntarenas to the stunning islands of the Gulf of Nicoya, or they head south to discover more quiet beaches and natural reserves.

Coastal Charms of Jacó and Manuel Antonio

Moving south from Puntarenas, the coast becomes more rocky and gorgeous, with the towns of Jacó and

Manuel Antonio serving as some of Costa Rica's most popular and accessible beach resorts.

Jacó: Famous for its dynamic nightlife and surf culture, Jacó draws a diverse audience of beachgoers and surfers from all over the world. The town is also a hub for adventure activities such as ATV trips, horseback riding, and zip-lining.

Manuel Antonio: Manuel Antonio National Park, one of Costa Rica's most popular tourist destinations, combines lush jungle with white-sand beaches and coral reefs. Wildlife in the park includes sloths, iguanas, uncommon birds, and numerous monkey species.

Eco-Tourism: Both Jacó and Manuel Antonio are eco-tourism hotspots, with guided nature trips that emphasize sustainability and conservation.

Accommodation Options: The area offers a variety of accommodations, including luxury resorts, eco-lodges, and budget hostels, appealing to all types of travelers.

Osa Peninsula and Corcovado National Park

As one travels further south, the Osa Peninsula marks the final frontier of Costa Rica's Pacific Coast—a site where the jungle meets the sea and nature is mostly wild.

Corcovado National Park: Known as one of the most ecologically intense regions on Earth, Corcovado provides outstanding animal viewing opportunities. This secluded park is only accessible by foot, boat, or tiny plane, which adds to its attraction and mystery.

Wildlife Expeditions: Visitors to Corcovado can go on guided excursions through the dense forests, which are home to all four Costa Rican monkey species, jaguars, tapirs, and several bird species.

Conservation Efforts: The park is a conservation hotspot in Costa Rica, serving as an essential home for numerous endangered species and a research base for scientists and conservationists alike.

Drake Bay: known for its quiet charm and breathtaking natural beauty, is a good starting point for exploring the northern regions of the Osa Peninsula. It provides a quieter alternative to the more touristic areas up north, with eco-friendly accommodations and a dedication to conserving its beautiful nature.

Drake Bay is a popular snorkeling and diving destination due to its clear waters and diverse marine life, especially around Caño Island, a protected marine reserve.

Cultural Insights and Sustainable Travel

Traveling to Southern Costa Rica allows you to not only see some of the country's most beautiful natural landscapes but also interact with local communities and participate in sustainable travel activities. Many lodges and tour operators in the region participate in community-led conservation efforts, which visitors can support by booking lodgings and activities.

Southern Costa Rica's Pacific Coast, from Puntarenas to Corcovado, captures the essence of a tropical paradise with a dash of adventure and a dedication to conservation. Whether you're exploring the lively streets of Puntarenas, surfing the waves at Jacó, basking in the natural splendor of Manuel Antonio, or trekking through the wild jungles of Corcovado, this region offers a variety of experiences for the adventurous spirit, nature lovers, and cultural explorers. Every traveler discovers their piece of Costa Rica, surrounded by the Pacific Coast's unrivaled beauty and vibrant culture.

Monteverde Cloud Forest: A Haven for Nature Lovers

Monteverde Cloud Forest Reserve, located in Costa Rica's Tilarán Mountain Range, is one of the planet's most stunning and ecologically diverse places. This mystical forest, marked by constant mist and deep, lush flora, serves as a beacon for environmentalists, biologists, and nature lovers from all over the world. Its distinct temperature and elevation have resulted in a biodiversity hotspot that is both sensitive and incredibly alive.

Monteverde's cloud forest is an ecosystem in which high humidity and regular cloud cover provide a wet, chilly climate that supports a varied range of flora and fauna. This natural area is distinguished by towering trees draped in mosses, ferns, and orchids, forming a green tapestry that extends as far as the eye can see.

Plants and Animals: Monteverde is home to approximately 2,500 plant species, including over

500 orchid varieties. The woodlands also provide a haven for several wildlife species, including the elusive Resplendent Quetzal, Three-wattled Bellbird, and a plethora of other bird species, making it a world-class bird-watching destination. Mammals like the jaguar, ocelot, and Baird's tapir live deeper within, while innumerable insects and an ever-present symphony of amphibians contribute to the forest's vivid life.

Explore the Monteverde Cloud Forest Reserve.

The Monteverde Cloud Forest Reserve, which spans over 10,500 hectares, is one of the world's most famous cloud forests due to its biodiversity, conservation efforts, and beauty, attracting people looking to immerse themselves in its tranquil and verdant scenery.

Hiking paths: The reserve has a well-kept network of paths that allow visitors to explore the heart of the cloud forest. Trails range in difficulty and duration, appealing to both experienced hikers seeking challenging paths and casual walkers looking for a calm stroll.

Guided Tours: To properly appreciate the cloud forest's complexity and splendor, guided tours are essential. Local specialists shed light on the ecological significance of what could otherwise be missed, as well as impart knowledge about the forest's delicate balance, pointing out hidden critters and plants.

Canopy Tours and Hanging Bridges: Canopy excursions and suspended bridges provide a fresh viewpoint of the forest. These trips offer not only thrilling experiences but also a unique perspective on life in the treetops.

Conservation Efforts and Environmental Education

Monteverde is a paradigm for effective conservation initiatives. The region has a long history of grassroots conservation projects spearheaded by both local and foreign experts. The Monteverde Conservation League and other organizations work ceaselessly to preserve and extend forested areas.

Sustainability: Eco-tourism is important in Monteverde, with many resorts and tour operators emphasizing environmental responsibility. The community strongly supports practices that reduce environmental impact and increase conservation education.

Research Opportunities: The reserve is also an important research location. Scientists and students from all over the world come to study its different ecosystems, adding to the expanding body of knowledge about cloud forests and climate change.

Community and Culture in Monteverde

Aside from its natural beauty, Monteverde is also noted for its diverse cultural tapestry. Descendants of American Quakers who settled in the area in the 1950s had a tremendous impact on local culture, encouraging peace and environmental conservation.

Art and Education: The town of Santa Elena, located near the reserve, has cultural attractions such as art galleries, craft shops, and coffee excursions that showcase the traditional Costa Rican way of life alongside influences from international citizens.

Culinary Scene: The area's restaurants are noted for employing local products to create both traditional Costa Rican and foreign food, reflecting the community's diverse character.

Visitor Info and Tips

When planning a trip to Monteverde, keep in mind that the high altitude and cloud cover make for a wetter, cooler environment. Layering and wearing waterproof gear can help make forest expeditions more comfortable and pleasurable.

Best Time to Visit: While Monteverde's weather is generally stable, the dry season, which runs from December to April, provides better skies and less rain, making it perfect for animal viewing and trekking.

Accommodations: range from rustic lodges with a focus on nature to more opulent hotels with modern conveniences, all designed to match the local terrain.

Monteverde Cloud Forest is more than simply a destination; it's an experience that captures the spirit of conservation, the excitement of discovery, and the tranquil beauty of one of the planet's oldest ecosystems. Monteverde provides an unforgettable voyage into a world suspended in clouds and lush foliage for nature lovers, adventure seekers, and those interested in learning about rich biodiversity and ecological principles.

National Parks & Reserves in Costa Rica.

Costa Rica is well known for its dedication to preserving its natural beauty and biodiversity. With more than 25% of its territory protected as national parks and reserves, the country provides several possibilities for visitors to immerse themselves in pristine landscapes and witness a diverse range of animals. This guide covers some of the most spectacular national parks and reserves that should be at the top of your vacation itinerary.

Corcovado National Park

Corcovado National Park, located on the Osa Peninsula, is often regarded as one of the world's most ecologically intensive areas. This remote and mountainous park covers 164 square miles and is home to a diverse range of biodiversity, including endangered species and various indigenous flora and animals.

Highlights:

Biodiversity: The park has 13 major ecosystems, including mangrove swamps, rainforests, palm groves, and beaches. Jaguars, pumas, scarlet macaws, tapirs, and four different monkey species live there.

Popular activities include hiking through the deep rainforest, guided animal tours, and overnight camping adventures. Boat cruises throughout the park's rivers and coastal areas offer additional views of the countryside and its residents.

Manuel Antonio National Park

Manuel Antonio National Park, one of Costa Rica's smallest but most popular, is located on the central Pacific coast near the town of Quepos. The park is known for its beautiful beaches, lush woods, and diverse fauna.

Highlights:

Beaches: Manuel Antonio has some of Costa Rica's most stunning beaches, with white sand and crystal blue waters perfect for swimming, snorkeling, and sunbathing.

Wildlife: Visitors can see sloths, capuchin monkeys, and several bird species. The park's well-marked trails allow easy access to a variety of environments, including coastal lagoons and evergreen woods.

Accessibility: The park is ideal for families and travelers searching for shorter, more accessible walks.

Arenal Volcanic National Park

The enormous Arenal Volcano dominates this national park in the Northern Plains, which provides spectacular vistas and thrilling outdoor activities. Although the volcano has been dormant since 2010, it is still a prominent landmark of the region.

Highlights:

Volcano Views: The park has various paths that provide amazing views of the volcano and its surrounding scenery. The Arenal 1968 Trail honors the huge eruption of that year.

Hot Springs: The geothermal activity in the area has resulted in numerous hot springs, which are ideal for unwinding after a long day of hiking.

Arenal is a destination for adventure activities such as zip-lining, white-water rafting, and canopy tours.

Monteverde Cloud Forest Reserve.

Monteverde Cloud Forest Reserve, known for its mist-covered trees and great biodiversity, is a naturalist's and birdwatcher's paradise. This high-altitude reserve is renowned for its distinct cloud forest ecosystems.

Highlights:

Biodiversity: The reserve is home to approximately 400 bird species, 100 animal species, and numerous plant species, including an incredible array of orchids.

Canopy trips: Visitors can explore the forest canopy with hanging bridges and zip-line trips, which provide a unique view of the ecosystem.

Conservation and Research: Monteverde is a hub for conservation initiatives and scientific research, with several educational trips available.

Tortuguero National Park

Tortuguero National Park, known as the "Amazon of Costa Rica," is a network of canals, rivers, and wetlands on the Caribbean coast. This park is an important breeding site for various species of sea turtles.

Highlights:

Turtle Nesting: From July to October, tourists can see the nesting of green sea turtles, which is a unique experience. Leatherback and hawksbill turtles both nest here.

Boat Tours: Boats are the ideal method to explore the park's waterways since they provide access to remote locations and the opportunity to see animals including manatees, caimans, and a variety of birds.

Tortuguero is home to jaguars, howler monkeys, sloths, and a diverse range of plants.

Rincon de la Vieja National Park.

Rincon de la Vieja National Park, located in the province of Guanacaste, is centered on the active Rincon de la Vieja volcano. The park's geothermal activity has resulted in a landscape of bubbling mud pots, hot springs, and fumaroles.

Highlights:

Volcanic Activity: The Las Pailas area has an impressive display of geothermal activity, including boiling mud pots and steaming vents.

Hiking routes: The park has many routes, including a popular walk to the summit of Rincon de la Vieja Volcano, which provides panoramic views of the surrounding environment.

Waterfalls and Hot Springs: Visitors can cool off in the park's waterfalls and relax in the natural hot springs.

Santa Rosa National Park

Santa Rosa, Costa Rica's first national park, was founded in 1971 and is significant both ecologically and historically. The park protects part of the world's last remaining tropical dry forest and honors the Battle of Santa Rosa, a watershed moment in Costa Rican history.

Highlights:

Historical Sites: La Casona, where the Battle of Santa Rosa took place, is now a museum and memorial to Costa Rica's independence war.

Biodiversity: The park is home to a wide range of wildlife, including howler monkeys, white-tailed deer, and numerous bird species.

Beaches: The park features beautiful beaches including Playa Naranjo, which is famed for its surfing waves and quiet beauty.

Cahuita National Park.

Cahuita National Park, located on the Caribbean coast, is recognized for its coral reefs, black sand beaches, and vibrant Afro-Caribbean culture. The park provides good chances for snorkeling and animal observation.

Highlights:

Coral Reefs: The park's coral reefs are among the most vibrant in Costa Rica, supporting a diverse range of marine life, including colorful fish and sea turtles.

Wildlife: Howler monkeys, sloths, and raccoons live in the park on land, while sea turtles and a variety of bird species can be seen along the coast.

Cultural Significance: Cahuita's Afro-Caribbean community enriches the park experience by allowing visitors to enjoy local music, food, and traditions.

Sustainable Tourism and Responsible Travel

Costa Rica's dedication to conservation extends to the tourism sector. Visitors are encouraged to use sustainable practices to help preserve the country's natural beauty. Tips for Responsible Travel:

Eco-Friendly Lodging: Select accommodations that prioritize sustainability, such as eco-lodges and hotels with environmental certifications.

Respect wildlife: Keep a safe distance from animals, avoid feeding them, and adhere to recommendations to reduce your influence on natural environments.

Minimise rubbish: Use reusable water bottles and bags and dispose of rubbish correctly.

Support Local Communities: Buy locally produced goods and services to help the economies of the places you visit.

Costa Rica's national parks and reserves are more than just tourist sites; they are essential ecosystems that contribute significantly to global biodiversity.

Exploring these natural beauties allows you to interact with the environment, learn about conservation, and enjoy Costa Rica's spectacular beauty. Whether you're hiking through lush rainforests, snorkeling in vivid coral reefs, or admiring volcanic scenery, these protected places provide remarkable experiences and a deep appreciation for the natural world.

Volcanoes and Hot Springs: Exploring Arenal, Poás, and Irazú

Costa Rica is a region of spectacular landscapes and geothermal wonders, where majestic volcanoes tower over lush jungles and soothing hot springs entice visitors seeking relaxation and refreshment. Arenal, Poás, and Irazú volcanoes are among of the country's most popular natural attractions. Each of these behemoths provides distinct experiences, ranging from thrilling hikes and spectacular views to relaxing hot springs that reflect the essence of Costa Rica's volcanic splendor.

Arenal Volcano

Arenal Volcano, one of Costa Rica's most recognizable sights, rises 1,657 meters (5,437 feet) amid the Northern Plains. Arenal, once one of the world's most active volcanoes, has been at rest since 2010. However, its precisely conical shape and surrounding surroundings continue to draw visitors from all over the world.

Hiking, Exploration:

Arenal Volcano National Park has a range of paths suitable for hikers of all skill levels. The Los Heliconias and Las Coladas trails are particularly popular, offering breathtaking views of the volcano and its lava fields. Hikers can explore secondary forests and open fields, where they can see wildlife and unusual plant species.

Arenal 1968 walk: Named after the huge eruption of 1968, this walk features lush vegetation and lava rock formations, as well as panoramic views of the volcano and Arenal Lake.

Hot springs

Tabacón Grand Spa Thermal Resort is a magnificent resort with natural hot springs supplied by Arenal Volcano's geothermal activity. Visitors can rest in mineral-rich thermal pools surrounded by tropical plants.

Eco Termales Hot Springs: Known for its private setting, Eco Termales provides a tranquil escape with various thermal pools and a commitment to sustainability.

Baldi Hot Springs: With its numerous pools, waterslides, and lush scenery, Baldi is ideal for families and people looking for a fun, relaxing getaway.

Adventure Activities

Zip-Lining: Several companies provide exhilarating zip-line experiences with bird's-eye views of the forest canopy and volcano.

White-Water Rafting: The local rivers, such as the Balsa and Toro, provide exhilarating rafting opportunities for all ability levels.

Horseback Riding: Enjoy guided trips through forests and open fields as you explore the gorgeous area around Arenal on horseback.

Poás Volcano

Poás Volcano, located in the Central Valley, stands at 2,708 meters (8,885 feet) and is one of Costa Rica's most accessible active volcanoes. Poás, famous for its enormous crater and brilliant blue-green acidic lake, provides a readily accessible adventure with spectacular landscapes.

Visitor Experience:

Poás Volcano National Park has well-maintained pathways that lead directly to the crater overlook. The main crater, one of the world's largest, is awe-inspiring with its steamy fumaroles and sulfurous lake. Laguna Botos, a subsidiary crater, is a cool, rain-fed lake encircled by a cloud forest that offers a peaceful contrast to the active crater.

Educational Centre: The park's visitor center features displays on the volcano's geology, history, and surrounding ecosystem. Rangers are accessible to offer insights and answer questions.

Hiking trails:

Crater Rim walk: This short walk goes to numerous vistas around the main crater, providing excellent photographic opportunities.

Laguna Botos Trail: A modest walk through the cloud forest leads to the peaceful Laguna Botos. The trail is rich in biodiversity, providing opportunities to observe rare plant and animal species.

Nearby attractions

La Paz Waterfall Gardens: Just a short drive from Poás, this private reserve boasts breathtaking waterfalls, a butterfly observatory, and beautiful gardens teeming with tropical flora and fauna.

Coffee Plantations: The excellent soils surrounding Poás are ideal for coffee cultivation. Tours of local coffee farms, such as Doka Estate, provide insights into the entire coffee production process, from bean to cup.

Irazú Volcano

Costa Rica's highest active volcano, Irazú Volcano, is at 3,432 meters (11,260 ft). Irazú, located in the Central Highlands near Cartago, has panoramic views of the Pacific and Atlantic Oceans on clear days.

Visitor Experience:

The Irazú Volcano National Park is easily accessible by car, with paved roads up to the summit. The major attraction is the Diego de la Haya crater, which is famous for its eerie, moon-like environment and the ever-changing color of its crater lake, which ranges from emerald green to grey depending on volcanic activity and weather.

Observation Decks: Several vantage points around the crater offer panoramic views of the surrounding environment and the Central Valley. Clear days reveal the shape of Nicaragua's Lake Managua to the north and the Caribbean coast to the east.

Hiking, Exploration:

Crater routes: Although the major routes are short and easy, they provide spectacular vistas and close contact with the volcanic nature. Irazú has pathways for all ages and fitness levels, making it an ideal location for families.

Irazú's high-altitude habitat supports both alpine vegetation and tropical highland forest. The park's pathways provide an opportunity to explore these unique ecosystems.

Nearby attractions

Cartago City: Cartago, Costa Rica's former capital, has a rich history and culture. Visit the Basilica of Our Lady of the Angels, a pilgrimage site with stunning architecture and deep religious significance.

Orosi Valley: is a lovely valley famed for its natural beauty, coffee plantations, and ancient remains. The valley provides additional trekking options and breathtaking scenery.

Benefits of Volcanic Hot Springs

Costa Rica's volcanic activity not only impacts the environment but also produces natural hot springs with medicinal properties. Mineral-rich waters are said to promote circulation, lower tension, and alleviate muscle discomfort. The hot springs of Arenal, Poás, and Irazú offer travelers a pleasant respite.

Sustainable Tourism and Conservation

Costa Rica's dedication to sustainability includes its volcanic regions and hot springs. Many national parks and hot spring resorts use environmentally friendly measures to reduce their influence on the environment. Visitors are advised to adhere to Leave No Trace principles, support local conservation initiatives, and select accommodations and tour operators who prioritize sustainability.

Exploring Costa Rica's volcanoes and hot springs provides a unique combination of adventure, natural beauty, and relaxation. Discover memorable adventures at Arenal Volcano, Poás, and Irazú. Whether you're hiking through volcanic landscapes, swimming in mineral-rich waters, or learning about geothermal activity, these sites embody Costa Rica's dynamic nature and commitment to conservation. Explore these geothermal wonders and discover Costa Rica's transformational power of nature.

Costa Rica Beaches

Costa Rica's Pacific Coast is famous for its beautiful beaches, each offering a distinct experience that caters to a wide range of interests, from surfing and snorkeling to animal watching and sunbathing. These beaches, which stretch from the lush woods of Manuel Antonio to the colorful town of Tamarindo, are not just places to relax, but also doorways to discovering Costa Rica's natural beauty and rich cultural heritage. Here's a complete guide to some of the most beautiful beaches in Costa Rica.

Manuel Antonio

Manuel Antonio, on Costa Rica's central Pacific coast, has some of the country's most magnificent beaches, surrounded by lush woods and colorful animals. The area is part of the Manuel Antonio National Park, which is known for its biodiversity and clean shoreline.

Playa Manuel Antonio:

Scenic Beauty: This beach is known for its smooth white sands and crystal-clear waves, which are set against the backdrop of a lush jungle. The stunning scenery makes it an ideal location for photography and leisure.

Wildlife Watching: The nearby national park is alive with wildlife. Visitors can see capuchin monkeys, sloths, and a variety of bird species directly on the shore. It is not uncommon to witness monkeys playing on the beach or toucans swooping overhead.

Playa Manuel Antonio's tranquil seas are great for swimming, snorkeling, and kayaking. The coral reefs along the beach provide a glimpse into the area's diverse aquatic life.

Playa Espadilla:

Surfing and Sunbathing: Playa Espadilla, next to Playa Manuel Antonio, is a longer stretch of beach with terrific waves for surfing and plenty of space for sunbathing. Beginners can take instruction at surf schools along the beach.

Local Amenities: Vendors surround the beach, selling refreshing drinks, local delicacies, and equipment rentals. It's a bustling location with a dynamic atmosphere.

Dominical: The Surf Haven.

Dominical, located south of Manuel Antonio, is a little beach town known for its tremendous surf and relaxed atmosphere. Dominical attracts surfers from all over the world, providing a more rural and less crowded alternative to more established beach communities.

Playa Dominical:

Surfing: Dominical is one of Costa Rica's greatest surfing destinations thanks to its constant, strong waves. Surfers of all skill levels can find acceptable waves, with surf schools accessible for novices.

Beachfront Charm: The beach town maintains a bohemian vibe, with local artisans, beach bars, and cafes contributing to the laid-back ambiance.

Yoga and Wellness: Dominical also hosts yoga and wellness retreats. Several coastal venues offer yoga sessions and holistic therapies, making it an ideal getaway for anyone looking to unwind and rejuvenate.

Playa Dominicalito:

Playa Dominicalito, located just south of Playa Dominical, with calmer surf and a more relaxed atmosphere. It's ideal for people who prefer a more peaceful beach experience or want a safer place for beginner surfers.

Uvita and Marino Ballena National Park

Continuing south, Uvita is famed for its beautiful beaches and the distinctive Whale's Tail formation at Marino Ballena National Park. This region is not only physically appealing, but it also provides excellent opportunities for encounters with aquatic life.

Playa Uvita:

Whale viewing: Humpback whales migrate through the area twice a year, making it a popular whale viewing destination. Tours depart often, allowing tourists to see these gorgeous creatures up close.

Whale's Tail Formation: During low tide, the distinctive Whale's Tail sandbar appears, allowing tourists to walk out onto the formation. It's a breathtaking site and a favorite photography location.

Snorkeling and Diving: The pristine waters surrounding the Whale's Tail are ideal for snorkeling and diving, with vivid coral reefs and a diverse marine population.

Playa Hermosa:

Family-Friendly Beach: Playa Hermosa, located north of Uvita, has calmer waters and large sandy shores, making it excellent for families to swim. The beach is also an excellent place to picnic and watch sunsets.

Sámara: The Laid-Back Beach Town

Moving north to the Nicoya Peninsula, Sámara is a quaint beach town known for its laid-back vibe and inviting inhabitants. The beach here is ideal for a variety of activities, appealing to both adventurers and those wishing to relax.

Playa sámara:

Safe Swimming: Playa Sámara's gentle waves and shallow seas make it a safe and fun swimming spot, particularly for families with children.

Water sports: on the beach include kayaking, paddle boarding, and snorkeling. Local operators offer equipment rental and guided tours.

Local Culture: The town of Sámara is alive with local culture, which combines Costa Rican traditions with worldwide influences. Visitors can sample local cuisine, music, and art in the town's numerous restaurants and galleries.

Playa Carillo:

Secluded Beauty: Playa Carrillo, located south of Sámara, is one of Costa Rica's most beautiful and least congested beaches. The palm-lined beach and clean sands create a lovely environment for relaxation.

Fishing and boating: The calm seas make it an excellent location for fishing and boating. Visitors can organize fishing charters or boat cruises to explore the shoreline.

Tamarindo: The Bustling Beach Town

Tamarindo, in Guanacaste province, is one of Costa Rica's most popular beach resorts. Tamarindo, known for its active nightlife, superb surf, and numerous food options, caters to everyone.

Playa Tamarindo:

Surfing: Tamarindo is known for its consistent surf breaks, which draw surfers of all levels. Surf schools and rental businesses are plentiful, making it simple for newcomers to surf the waves.

Nightlife & Dining: The town is well-known for its vibrant nightlife, which includes a variety of bars, clubs, and restaurants serving anything from local Costa Rican meals to foreign cuisine.

Shopping and Activities: Tamarindo has a diverse range of businesses, from local crafts to high-end boutiques. Visitors can engage in activities such as horseback riding, ATV trips, and sunset cruises.

Playa Langosta:

calm Escape: Playa Langosta, just south of Tamarindo, provides a more calm beach experience. It's an ideal location for a peaceful day of sunbathing, beachcombing, and watching the sunset.

Wildlife Viewing: The neighboring estuary is home to a variety of bird species and other wildlife, making it an ideal destination for nature lovers.

Sustainable Tourism and Responsible Travel

Costa Rica's beaches are not only stunning but also environmentally significant. The country's dedication to sustainability extends to its coastal areas, where measures are being taken to conserve marine life and ecosystems.

Marine Conservation: Many beaches, particularly those located within national parks and protected areas, are important breeding grounds for sea turtles. Visitors are invited to take part in conservation efforts, such as turtle nesting excursions, which benefit local preservation organizations.

Eco-Friendly Practices: When visiting these beaches, it is critical to engage in eco-friendly behaviors such as avoiding single-use plastics, picking up litter, and respecting the local species and habitats.

Supporting Local Communities: Choosing locally owned hotels, dining at local restaurants, and shopping with local craftsmen all contribute to boosting coastal communities' economies and promoting sustainable tourism.

From the beautiful jungles of Manuel Antonio to the colorful town of Tamarindo, Costa Rica's Pacific Coast has a plethora of stunning beaches, each with its distinct character and attractions. Whether you're looking for adventure, leisure, wildlife encounters, or cultural activities, these beaches make the ideal setting for an amazing journey. Embrace the natural beauty, immerse yourself in local culture, and participate in the numerous activities that make Costa Rica's beaches so magnificent.

Wildlife and Nature Tours

Costa Rica is a nature lover's dream, with a diverse range of ecosystems supporting an incredible variety of species. The country's commitment to conservation has resulted in the protection of enormous sections of rainforest, cloud forests, wetlands, and coastal habitats, making it a top destination for wildlife and nature tourism. From bird viewing and guided jungle hikes to marine explorations and midnight safaris, Costa Rica provides numerous opportunities for close experiences with its spectacular animals and flora.

Bird Watching

Costa Rica is a top site for bird watching, with over 900 bird species. The country's diverse habitats, from lowland rainforests to highland cloud forests, support a diverse range of birds, many of which are indigenous or migratory.

Monteverde Cloud Forest Reserve.

The Resplendent Quetzal is one of the most sought-after birds that can be found in Monteverde. This bird, with its vivid green plumage and startling crimson belly, represents both beauty and mysticism.

Hummingbirds: Monteverde is particularly known for its hummingbird gardens, where you may see these small, colorful birds up close. Special feeders attract a variety of birds, creating fantastic photographic possibilities.

Carara National Park:

Scarlet Macaws: This park is a great site to see the majestic Scarlet Macaws. These huge, colorful parrots are frequently seen flying together or grazing in the treetops.

Diverse Birdlife: Carara's transitional forest, which bridges the dry and wet climates, supports a diverse range of bird species, making it a popular destination for dedicated birders.

Osa Peninsula and Corcovado National Park.

Endemic Species: The secluded Osa Peninsula is home to several rare bird species. Guided trips in Corcovado provide opportunities to see birds such as the Black-cheeked Ant-Tanager and the Turquoise Cotinga.

Waterbirds and Raptors: The park's coastal sections and marshes are also home to a variety of waterbirds and raptors, making for a unique birding experience.

Jungle Trekking and Rainforest Adventures

Exploring Costa Rica's vast jungles and rainforests provides opportunities to see some of the planet's most fascinating animals. Guided hikes into these deep forests give insights into the diverse ecosystems and the hidden lives of several creatures.

Arenal Volcano National Park.

Mammals and Reptiles: The trails surrounding Arenal Volcano are filled with wildlife. Watch out for coatis, peccaries, and numerous monkey species. The park is also home to a variety of snakes and reptiles.

Arenal Hanging Bridges: This network of suspension bridges provides a unique view of the rainforest canopy, allowing you to see howler monkeys, sloths, and a variety of birds.

Tortuguero National Park:

Turtle breeding Tours: Tortuguero is well-known for its sea turtle breeding beaches. Guided night tours allow you to see green sea turtles, leatherbacks, and hawksbills deposit their eggs on the beach.

Canal Tours: Exploring Tortuguero's canal network by boat or kayak provides close encounters with caimans, river otters, and a diverse range of bird species.

Manuel Antonio National Park:

Accessible Wildlife Viewing: Manuel Antonio is noted for its friendly fauna. The park's well-kept trails make it possible to spot sloths, iguanas, and a variety of monkey species, including the endangered squirrel monkey.

Guided Tours: Hiring a local guide can substantially enhance your trip by giving professional information and identifying creatures that might otherwise go unnoticed.

Marine Exploration and Coastal Adventure

Costa Rica's coastal waters and marine parks provide several opportunities to discover underwater life and observe marine creatures. Whether snorkeling, diving, or going on a whale-watching excursion, the marine biodiversity is just as stunning as the land-based animals.

Caño Island Biological Reserve:

Snorkeling and Diving: Caño Island's waters are home to a diverse range of marine life, including rays, sharks, and fish. Coral reefs create bright underwater landscapes ideal for snorkeling and diving.

Whale and Dolphin Watching: Tours frequently see humpback whales, particularly during migration seasons, as well as playful dolphins that live in the area year-round.

Golfo dulce:

Golfo Dulce is a unique, enclosed gulf with calm waters that serves as a nursery for a wide variety of marine creatures. It's a great place to view dolphins and see the rare whale sharks.

Mangrove trips: Kayak trips through the mangroves show a distinct aspect of marine life, such as diverse bird species, crabs, and the occasional crocodile.

Marine Ballena National Park:

Whale's Tail Formation: Named for its unusual whale tail-shaped sandbar, this park is a great place to see humpback whales. During tours, these massive creatures frequently breach and play in the water.

Snorkeling: The park's pristine waters and protected coral reefs make it an ideal snorkeling destination, with opportunities to observe turtles, tropical fish, and rays.

Nocturnal Safaris: Exploring Nightlife.

Costa Rica's midnight safaris provide a whole different view of the country's wildlife. As night sets, a new group of monsters emerges, delivering a fresh and fascinating experience.

Monteverde Night Walks:

Nighttime Activity: Many Costa Rican creatures are nocturnal. Night hikes in Monteverde reveal armadillos, kinkajous, and a variety of insects and amphibians.

Guided Tours: Experienced guides utilize spotlights to discover and identify wildlife, allowing you to make the most of your nighttime excursion.

La Fortuna Night Tours:

Frog Watching: The surroundings surrounding La Fortuna are well-known for their various frog populations. Night tours frequently feature colorful species such as the Poison Dart Frog and the Red-eyed Tree Frog.

Owl & Bat Spotting: These tours allow you to spot nocturnal birds and bats, giving you a complete picture of the area's evening biodiversity.

Osa Peninsula Night Hikes:

Wild Encounters: The secluded Osa Peninsula provides some of the best nocturnal animal experiences. Night hikes through Corcovado can expose elusive species such as pumas, tapirs, and other nocturnal birds and reptiles.

Conservation and Responsible Tourism.

Costa Rica's wildlife and environment tours are inextricably linked with the country's conservation efforts. Sustainable tourism practices are critical to ensuring that these natural beauties are preserved for future generations.

Eco-Friendly Practices: Tour operators and guides promote environmentally friendly practices such as carrying reusable water bottles, avoiding single-use plastics, and preserving wildlife habitats.

Supporting Local Communities: Many wildlife trips are operated by local communities, which provides them with a steady income while also advocating the preservation of natural resources. Choosing locally owned tours helps to support these efforts while also fostering a stronger connection to the area.

Education and Awareness: Many tours include educational components that teach guests about ecosystems, conservation initiatives, and the value of biodiversity preservation. This raises awareness and encourages a conservation culture among travelers.

Costa Rica's wildlife and environment tours provide unequaled possibilities for close interactions with some of the most spectacular creatures and scenery on the planet. Explore the bird-rich cloud forests of Monteverde, the marine biodiversity of Caño Island, the nighttime wonders of the Osa Peninsula, and the approachable wildlife of Manuel Antonio. These encounters are both exhilarating and instructive. Visitors may enjoy these natural treasures while also helping to preserve them, ensuring that Costa Rica remains a beacon of biodiversity and a model for sustainable travel. Whether you are an avid birdwatcher, a marine enthusiast, or simply a nature lover, Costa Rica offers amazing experiences that appreciate the natural world's beauty and diversity.

Activities and Tours in Costa Rica

Costa Rica is a playground for both adventurers and nature lovers, with a wide selection of activities to suit everyone's interests. Whether you're hiking through lush rainforests, catching the perfect wave, photographing unusual birds, or seeking inner peace at a yoga retreat, this dynamic country offers endless possibilities to explore and appreciate its natural treasures. Here is a detailed reference to some of Costa Rica's most popular activities and tours.

Hiking and Trekking in Costa Rica

Costa Rica's various landscapes provide some of the most scenic and enjoyable hiking and trekking opportunities in the world. From volcanic routes to deep rainforests and cloud forests, there's plenty for every hiking skill level.

Arenal Volcano National Park.

Hiking paths: The park has several paths suitable for hikers of all abilities. The Las Coladas walk leads you through historic lava fields and provides close-up views of the volcano and Arenal Lake. The El Ceibo walk winds through secondary woodland, passing a large Ceibo tree.

Wildlife Viewing: Hikers frequently see howler monkeys, white-faced capuchins, and a variety of bird species. The park's biodiversity enhances the trekking experience.

Monteverde Cloud Forest Reserve.

Cloud Forest paths: Monteverde's paths take you through one of the world's most famous cloud forests. The Sendero Bosque Nuboso (Cloud Forest Trail) is a strenuous walk with stunning vistas of rich foliage and unique fauna.

Hanging Bridges: The reserve has multiple suspension bridges that allow you to explore the

111

forest canopy, giving you unusual viewpoints and the opportunity to see canopy-dwelling species.

Corcovado National Park.

Corcovado is known for its remote and steep terrain, making it suitable for experienced trekkers seeking adventure. The Sirena Ranger Station serves as a primary location for multi-day excursions through the park's different habitats.

Corcovado is one of the most biodiverse regions on the earth, with animals such as jaguars, tapirs, and scarlet macaws. Guided tours are suggested for navigating the park's difficult paths and maximizing wildlife observations.

Rincón de La Vieja National Park:

Volcanic Landscapes: The park's paths include a variety of volcanic characteristics, such as bubbling mud pots, fumaroles, and hot springs. The walk to the summit of Rincón de la Vieja Volcano offers panoramic views of the surrounding area.

Waterfalls and Hot Springs: Trails like the Las Pailas loop lead to picturesque waterfalls and natural hot springs, ideal for a refreshing soak after a walk.

Surfing and Watersports

Costa Rica is known for its world-class surfing and water sports. The country's large coastline, with beaches facing both the Pacific Ocean and the Caribbean Sea, provides ideal conditions for a wide range of water activities.

Tamarindo:

Tamarindo is one of Costa Rica's most popular surfing spots, recognized for its consistent waves and strong surf culture. Surf schools and rental shops border the beach, catering to both new and experienced surfers.

Other water sports available in Tamarindo include stand-up paddleboarding, kayaking, and snorkeling. The Tamarindo Estuary is ideal for wildlife expeditions by kayak.

Jaco:

Surfing and Nightlife: Jaco is another popular surfing location, with beach breakers appropriate for all skill levels. The town's vibrant nightlife and several surf shops make it a popular destination for younger visitors.

Adventure rides: In addition to surfing, Jaco provides a variety of adventure activities such as ATV rides, zip line, and deep sea fishing.

Nosara:

Surf and Yoga: Nosara combines great surfing with a strong emphasis on wellbeing. Playa Guiones is known for its consistent waves, which are ideal for surfers of all skill levels. The town also has various yoga retreats and wellness centers.

Eco-Friendly Vibe: Nosara's commitment to sustainability, combined with its laid-back ambiance, make it an ideal destination for environmentally aware travelers.

Puerto Viejo:

Caribbean Surfing: On the Caribbean coast, Puerto Viejo's Salsa Brava has some of Costa Rica's largest and most powerful waves. It's a difficult place best suited to advanced surfers.

Snorkeling and Diving: The adjacent Cahuita National Park offers excellent snorkeling and diving options, with vivid coral reefs and diverse marine life.

Birdwatching and Wildlife Photography

Costa Rica's rich biodiversity makes it an ideal destination for birdwatchers and wildlife photographers. The country's diverse environments sustain an incredible range of species, providing several opportunities for intimate encounters and breathtaking images.

Monteverde Cloud Forest Reserve.

Monteverde is a popular bird-watching site with over 400 species, including the Resplendent Quetzal,

Three-wattled Bellbird, and a variety of hummingbirds.

Photography Tours: Guided tours can enhance your experience by providing professional advice on the best locations and times to photograph the diverse avian population.

Carara National Park:

Scarlet Macaws: Carara is a great site to see the stunning Scarlet Macaw. The park's various ecosystems support a diverse range of bird species, making it a popular bird-watching destination.

Accessible paths: The park's well-kept paths allow visitors to easily explore and photograph its species, which include colorful birds, reptiles, and mammals.

Osa Peninsula and Corcovado National Park.

Diverse Wildlife: Corcovado is a wildlife photographer's paradise, with the opportunity to catch classic animals such as jaguars, tapirs, and monkeys. The park's secluded location and diverse wildlife make it an attractive destination for serious photographers.

Night Photography: Nocturnal trips allow you to shoot species such as the red-eyed tree frog, bats, and other nocturnal mammals.

Tortuguero National Park:

Turtle Nesting: Tortuguero is known for its sea turtle nesting locations. Guided night trips offer the opportunity to shoot these wonderful creatures as they lay eggs.

Canal Tours: Exploring Tortuguero's canals by boat provides unique vistas and opportunities for photographing a variety of animals, including caimans, toucans, and howler monkeys.

Yoga Retreats and Wellness Centres

Costa Rica's natural beauty and calm surroundings make it an ideal location for yoga retreats and wellness centers. These retreats provide holistic experiences that incorporate yoga, meditation, and wellness techniques within the country's breathtaking scenery.

Nosara:

Yoga Capital: Nosara is recognized as Costa Rica's yoga capital, with various retreats and wellness centers. The Nosara Yoga Institute and Bodhi Tree Yoga Resort are two of the most well-known, providing comprehensive programs for students of various skill levels.

Many retreats in Nosara provide a holistic approach to well-being, which includes nutrition, detox programs, and spa treatments. The town's eco-friendly vibe contributes to the whole experience.

Santa Teresa:

Beachfront Yoga: Santa Teresa's magnificent beaches and relaxed ambiance make it a perfect destination for yoga retreats. Many centers provide beachfront sessions, allowing students to practice with the sound of the ocean in the background.

Surf and Yoga: Surfing and yoga are popular in Santa Teresa, and several retreats provide packages that include both activities.

Punta Mona:

Off-grid Retreats: Punta Mona is a permaculture farm and retreat center on the Caribbean coast. It provides immersive experiences in sustainable living, permaculture, and yoga, creating a one-of-a-kind and transformative retreat experience.

communal Focus: Punta Mona's retreats emphasize communal living and connection with nature, creating a friendly and enriching environment for all participants.

Blue Spirit Retreat in Nosara:

Blue Spirit is one of Costa Rica's most prestigious retreat centers, with a diverse choice of programs offered by world-class instructors. The center's breathtaking location overlooking the Pacific Ocean creates a tranquil and inspiring environment for yoga and meditation.

Comprehensive Wellness: Blue Spirit's programs frequently incorporate workshops on nutrition, mindfulness, and personal development, making it a holistic retreat location.

Accepting Sustainability in Activities and Tours

Costa Rica's dedication to sustainability extends to its adventure and health programs. Many travel operators and retreat centers prioritize environmentally responsible techniques.

Eco-Friendly Tours: Select tours and activities that follow sustainable principles, such as reducing waste, using environmentally friendly transportation, and supporting conservation initiatives.

Local Community Support: Supporting locally owned companies and tour operators encourages economic growth in communities while also encouraging sustainable tourist practices.

Leave No Trace: Whether hiking, surfing, or practicing yoga, always adhere to Leave No Trace principles to protect the natural beauty and integrity of the locations you visit.

Costa Rica has a variety of activities to suit a wide range of interests, including trekking through beautiful rainforests and surfing world-class waves, as well as bird watching and health retreats. The country's various landscapes and abundant wildlife offer limitless chances for adventure and relaxation. Visitors can enjoy these experiences while also helping to protect Costa Rica's natural wonders by adopting sustainable tourism practices. Whether you're looking for thrills, tranquility, or a deeper connection with nature, Costa Rica offers unique activities and fascinating encounters that reflect the country's beauty and diversity.

Local Crafts and Shopping

Costa Rica is well-known for its breathtaking scenery and abundant biodiversity, but it also has a vibrant culture that is represented in its local crafts and artisanal items. Whether you're meandering through crowded markets, visiting quiet artisan stores, or attending cultural events, you'll come across a variety of unique and wonderfully produced objects that represent the soul of Costa Rica. Bringing home a piece of this wonderful country helps you to preserve your memories while also supporting local craftspeople. Here's a detailed list of the greatest souvenirs to bring home from Costa Rica.

Traditional crafts and artisanal souvenirs

Handcrafted jewellery: Natural materials commonly used in Costa Rican jewelry include seeds, shells, wood, and volcanic rocks. Artisans expertly blend these components to create gorgeous works that capture the country's natural splendor.

Many local craftspeople employ bamboo jewelry, which is a sustainable resource. You can buy earrings, bracelets, and necklaces that are both lightweight and environmentally friendly.

Macrame and Beaded Jewellery: Costa Rican jewelry features intricate macrame and beaded patterns. These objects are frequently created by local artists, making each one distinctive.

Boruca Masks: The Indigenous Boruca people are noted for their colorful, hand-carved masks. These masks, which are typically worn during the annual Danza de los Diablitos celebration, show a variety of animal and spirit characters and are painted in vibrant colors.

Cultural value: Boruca masks are more than just decorative; they have cultural and historical value. Each mask conveys a tale and symbolizes the Boruca people's heritage and relationship to nature.

Where to Buy: To acquire real masks directly from artisans, visit Boruca village or local markets in San José and the surrounding areas.

Woodcrafts: Costa Rica is home to numerous expert woodworkers who create exquisite things out of locally obtained woods including teak, cedar, and Rosewood.

Carved Figurines: Animal figurines, particularly those of Costa Rican animals such as sloths, toucans, and jaguars, are popular gifts.

Decorative Bowls and Utensils: Wooden bowls, serving utensils, and chopping boards are not only utilitarian but also visually appealing.

Coffee and Coffee Accessories:

Costa Rican coffee is well-known for its quality and flavor. Coffee connoisseurs should always bring home a bag of locally farmed coffee beans.

Gourmet Coffee: Buy coffee from recognized manufacturers like Café Britt, which gives tours of its plantation and roasting facility.

Chorreador: This traditional Costa Rican coffee maker, made up of a wooden stand and a cloth filter, is a delightful and useful keepsake for coffee enthusiasts.

Pottery

The Chorotega people of the Nicoya Peninsula are well-known for their pottery, which is made using old skills passed down through generations.

Ceramic Vessels: These handcrafted objects frequently incorporate complicated geometric designs and natural hues. Vases, bowls, and plates are popular options.

Where to Buy: Visit Guaitil, a Chorotega pottery hub, to witness artisans at work and buy authentic pieces.

Textiles:

Costa Rican textiles are vibrant and colorful, highlighting the country's rich cultural past. Traditional materials and garments make great mementos.

Hand-woven bags created from natural fibers and embellished with traditional patterns are both functional and fashionable.

Sarongs and wraps: These adaptable pieces can serve as beach cover-ups, scarves, or ornamental throws.

Unique Shopping Destinations

San Jose:

The capital city provides a wide range of shopping experiences, from busy markets to luxury boutiques.

Mercado Central: This bustling market offers a wide range of local goods, including fresh vegetables, spices, crafts, and souvenirs. It's an excellent place to learn about local culture and find one-of-a-kind souvenirs.

Visit the Mercado de Artesanías and National Artisan Market to find unique handcrafted items. You can buy directly from artists here, assuring that the products are real and of great quality.

Sarchí:

Sarchí, the birthplace of Costa Rican handicrafts, is well-known for its colorful oxcarts and other woodcrafts.

Oxcarts: These traditional carts, called carretas, are decorated with intricate motifs and brilliant colors. Full-sized oxcarts are more of a collector's item, but miniature ones make excellent mementos.

Woodcraft Workshops: Visit local workshops to view craftspeople at work and make purchases straight from them. You'll find anything from furniture to decorations.

Monteverde:

Monteverde, with its temperate climate and rich scenery, is both a nature lover's paradise and a hub for one-of-a-kind crafts.

Local Artisans: The Monteverde Artisans Cooperative displays a diverse range of crafts, such as jewelry, pottery, and textiles. It's an excellent place to acquire one-of-a-kind goods while also supporting local artists.

Coffee Tours: Several coffee estates in the vicinity provide tours that conclude with a stop at their gift stores, where you can purchase fresh coffee and coffee-related gifts.

Caribbean coast:

The Caribbean coast of Costa Rica, notably the municipality of Puerto Viejo, has a distinct blend of Afro-Caribbean culture and crafts.

Rasta-Inspired Goods: The crafts represent the region's lively culture. Look for vibrant jewelry, clothing, and artwork influenced by Afro-Caribbean culture.

Local markets and roadside vendors offer homemade handicrafts, fresh spices, and locally created things.

The Nicoya Peninsula

The Nicoya Peninsula, famed for its stunning beaches and relaxed atmosphere, also has a variety of unique crafts.

Chorotega Pottery: As previously said, Guaitil is the place to go for authentic Chorotega pottery. You may see artists at work and make direct purchases from them.

Handmade Jewellery & Accessories: The Nicoya Peninsula's seaside villages, such as Tamarindo and Santa Teresa, are home to various stores providing handmade jewelry, beachwear, and other accessories.

Tips For Ethical Shopping

When shopping for souvenirs in Costa Rica, it is critical to do it ethically and environmentally. Here are some ways to make your purchases meaningful and responsible:

Buy Locally: Buying items manufactured by local artists not only assures that you are obtaining original products, but it also benefits the local economy. Look for fairs and businesses where you may purchase straight from the craftsmen.

Avoid mass-produced items: Avoid mass-produced goods marketed in tourist locations. These products are frequently imported and do not support the local population. Instead, look for one-of-a-kind, handmade things that celebrate Costa Rican culture and craftsmanship.

Look for fair trade certifications.

Some crafts and products may include fair trade certifications, showing that the artists are paid fairly and work in excellent conditions. Purchasing fair trade encourages ethical production techniques.

Respect wildlife: Avoid purchasing souvenirs made of endangered species or materials that harm nature.

This comprises things made of turtle shells, coral, and exotic animal parts.

Ask questions: Engage with the artisans and retailers. Inquire about the origins of the products and the procedures employed. This not only ensures that you are purchasing authentic things, but it also expands your knowledge of the trade and culture.

Negotiate fairly: Bargaining is frequent in markets, but do so respectfully. Remember that craftspeople rely on their craft for a living. Aim for reasonable pricing that reflects the effort and skill required to create the item.

Costa Rica's local crafts and artisanal products provide a unique window into the country's rich cultural legacy and natural beauty. From vivid Boruca masks and exquisite jewelry to world-renowned coffee and wonderfully produced pottery, there are plenty of significant gifts to take home. By purchasing responsibly and supporting local craftsmen, you not only get a piece of Costa Rica, but you also help to preserve and continue these traditional skills. Costa Rica's crafts will leave a lasting impact, whether you visit crowded marketplaces in San José, explore the artisan hamlet of Sarchí, or uncover hidden jewels along the coast.

Cultural experiences in Costa Rica.

Costa Rica has a rich cultural legacy, combining Indigenous traditions, Spanish colonial influences, and Afro-Caribbean components to create a vivid tapestry of experiences. Costa Rica's cultural landscape is as diverse as its natural splendor, ranging from the busy capital city of San José to rural indigenous settlements. This book explores the essence of Costa Rican culture and emphasizes the country's festivals and events, which provide a year-round schedule of celebrations and customs.

Costa Rican Culture

Costa Rican culture, sometimes known as "Tico culture," is defined by its warmth, friendliness, and great emphasis on family and community. This cultural identity is influenced by a combination of Indigenous roots, Spanish colonial history, and immigration from Europe, Africa, and Asia.

Pura Vida Philosophy: Costa Rican culture is centered on the word "Pura Vida," which translates to "pure life." This expression reflects the national spirit of enjoying life, being appreciative, and maintaining a cheerful outlook. It serves as a greeting, a farewell, and a response to the question "How are you?"

Indigenous heritage: Costa Rica has various Indigenous groups, including the Bribri, Boruca, Cabécar, and Maleku. These villages have retained their languages, crafts, and customs, which add to the country's cultural variety.

Bribri Community: The Bribri people live in the Talamanca region and practice traditional customs such as cocoa cultivation and shamanic rituals. Community-based tourism programs allow visitors to learn about the local way of life.

Boruca Masks: The Boruca people are famous for their beautifully carved and painted masks, which are used during the annual Danza de los Diablitos event.

These masks symbolize cultural endurance and artistic expression.

Spanish Colonial Influence: Costa Rica's architecture, language, and religion were all deeply influenced by Spanish colonization. Many towns and cities have colonial-era churches, plazas, and structures that reflect the period.

Cartago, Costa Rica's historic capital, is home to the Basilica of Our Lady of the Angels, a notable pilgrimage site for Catholics.

San José: The capital city has many specimens of colonial architecture, including the National Theatre and historic barrios like as Barrio Amón.

African-Caribbean Influence: The Caribbean coast, particularly the province of Limón, has a distinct Afro-Caribbean culture introduced by Jamaican immigrants in the nineteenth century. This impact is visible in the region's music, dancing, and cuisine.

Limón is known for its dynamic music culture, which includes genres like calypso, reggae, and salsa. Local musicians frequently play at festivals and community events.

Culinary Traditions: The local cuisine has a strong Afro-Caribbean flavor, including dishes such as coconut milk-cooked rice and beans, Rondon (a savory seafood stew), and patty (a spicy beef pastry).

Festivals and Events

Costa Rica's calendar is jam-packed with festivals and events honoring its diverse cultural heritage, religious traditions, and national pride. These events offer tourists an immersive experience, allowing them to see the country's many cultural expressions firsthand.

Palmares Festival, January: The Palmares Festival, one of Costa Rica's greatest and most popular celebrations, lasts two weeks and includes concerts, bullfights, horse parades, and traditional dances. This event, held in Palmares, attracts thousands of both locals and tourists.

Fiesta de los Diablitos (January/February): The Boruca community celebrates this Indigenous event in honor of their resistance to Spanish colonization. Participants perform ancient dances and ceremonies while wearing elaborate masks and costumes depicting devils.

Limon Carnival (October): The Limon Carnival, or Carnaval de Limón, is a lively celebration of Afro-Caribbean culture. The week-long celebration will feature colorful parades, live music, dancing performances, and street food kiosks.

Dia de los Muertos (November 1-2): Dia de los Muertos, often known as the Day of the Dead, is a traditional holiday that honors deceased loved ones. In Costa Rica, families go to cemeteries to clean and adorn graves with flowers, candles, and food offerings.

Fiestas de Zapote (December-January): The Fiestas de Zapote, which takes place in San José, is a colorful component of the Christmas and New Year celebrations. The event includes bullfighting (in a non-lethal variation in which the bulls are not hurt), fairground rides, concerts, and food booths.

Christmas and New Year's Celebrations: Christmas in Costa Rica is a family-oriented event that includes traditional delicacies such as tamales and festive decorations. The season concludes with New Year's Eve festivities, which include fireworks, parties, and San José's annual Tope Nacional horse parade.

Holy Week (Semana Santa, March/April): Semana Santa is one of Costa Rica's most prominent religious holidays. The week before Easter is commemorated by solemn processions, reenactments of Christ's Passion, and special church services.

Independence Day, September 15: Costa Rica's Independence Day is a patriotic event that includes parades, music, and dance performances. Schools and towns across the country take part in traditional festivities, such as the "lantern parade" (Desfile de Faroles), in which youngsters carry homemade lanterns.

Dia de la Virgen de Los Ángeles (August 2): This religious pilgrimage honors Costa Rica's patron saint, Virgen de los Ángeles. Thousands of pilgrims go from all over the country to the Basilica in Cartago to pay honor to the Virgin Mary.

Envision Festival (February): Envision is a one-of-a-kind festival that mixes music, art, yoga, and environmental sustainability. The event draws an international audience and focuses on holistic wellness and environmental consciousness.

Experiencing Costa Rican culture firsthand

To fully immerse yourself in Costa Rican culture, consider the following activities and experiences:

Homestay and Community-Based Tourism: Staying with rural families offers a real view of Costa Rican daily life. Community-based tourism efforts, such as those in the Bribri and Maleku communities, provide cultural tours, workshops, and traditional cuisine.

Cooking classes: Hands-on cooking lessons teach students how to prepare classic Costa Rican meals such as gallo pinto, casado, and tamales. Many cooking schools and local chefs provide programs that include trips to local markets to get fresh ingredients.

Dance and Music Lessons: Learn about Costa Rican culture via dance and music lessons. Learn to dance salsa, merengue, or cumbia, or take drum lessons to better grasp calypso and reggae rhythms.

Craft workshops: Attend workshops that teach traditional crafts including mask-making, ceramics, and weaving. These workshops not only provide a creative outlet but also help local craftspeople and protect cultural heritage.

Coffee and Chocolate Tours: Costa Rica is well known for its coffee and chocolate. Visit plantations and companies to learn about farming and production methods. These excursions frequently include samples and the opportunity to buy high-quality products straight from the source.

Language Classes: Improve your Spanish abilities by taking language lessons that focus on conversational practice and cultural immersion. Many schools have homestay alternatives, which allow you to live with a Costa Rican family while learning the language.

Costa Rica's rich cultural past is an important aspect of its character, providing visitors with a profound and engaging experience. Costa Rica's cultural experiences are as diverse as its natural landscapes, with the idea of "Pura Vida" and the rich traditions of Indigenous and Afro-Caribbean populations, as well as countless festivals celebrating religious and national pride.

Whether you attend local festivals, visit historical sites, or interact with artists and communities, you'll develop a deep respect for the traditions and values that distinguish this magnificent country. Accept the opportunity to engage with Costa Rican culture and bring back not only souvenirs but also memories and stories that will last a lifetime.

Travel Tips and Resources for Costa Rica

Costa Rica, noted for its lush surroundings, diverse wildlife, and kind people, is a dream destination for many travelers. To make the most of your stay, learn the local language and cultural customs. This guide contains useful linguistic hints and phrases, as well as crucial insights into Costa Rican cultural standards, to guarantee a pleasant and interesting vacation experience.

Language Tips and Essential Phrases

Spanish is Costa Rica's official language, and while English is widely spoken in tourist areas, knowing a little Spanish might improve your interactions and experiences. Here are some suggestions and words to help you communicate effectively during your vacation.

Basic Greetings and Polite Expressions:

- Hola: Hello

- Buenos días: Good morning
- Buenas tardes: Good afternoon
- Buenas noches: Good evening/night
- Adiós: Goodbye
- Hasta luego: See you later
- Por favor: Please
- Gracias: Thank you
- De nada: You're welcome
- Perdón: Excuse me/Sorry
- Sí: Yes
- No: No

Common Questions:

- Cómo está? How are you?
- Qué tal? How's it going?
- Cómo se llama? What is your name?
- De dónde es? Where are you from?
- Habla inglés? Do you speak English?
- Cuánto cuesta? How much does it cost?
- Dónde está...? Where is...?

Directions and Transportation:

- Dónde está el baño? Where is the bathroom?
- Cómo llego a...? How do I get to...?
- Quiero ir a... I want to go to...
- Una mesa para dos, por favor: A table for two, please
- A qué hora sale el autobús? What time does the bus leave?
- Cuánto cuesta el boleto? How much is the ticket?

At Restaurants and Cafés:

- La carta, por favor: The menu, please
- Quisiera... I would like...
- Qué me recomienda? What do you recommend?
- La cuenta, por favor: The check, please
- Sin hielo: No ice
- Con hielo: With ice

Emergencies and Health:

- Ayuda, por favor: Help, please
- Llame a la policía: Call the police
- Necesito un médico: I need a doctor
- Estoy perdido/a: I am lost
- Tengo alergia a... I am allergic to

Cultural Etiquette and Tips

Understanding and respecting local customs and etiquette is essential for having a great time in Costa Rica. Here are some cultural pointers to assist you in negotiating social situations and respecting the local way of life.

Greetings and Social Etiquette:

Handshake and Kiss: When welcoming someone, a light handshake and a cheek kiss (more of a cheek contact with a kissing sound) are frequent, particularly among women and men. Men usually shake hands.

To address someone older or in a formal environment, use titles like Señor (Mr.), Señora (Mrs.), or Señorita (Miss), followed by their last name.

Personal Space: Costa Ricans are generally kind and welcoming, but they also appreciate personal space. Respect physical boundaries by not touching strangers or standing too near.

Punctuality and Time Perception.

La Hora Tica: Costa Ricans have a relaxed approach to time, known as "La Hora Tica." Social events and gatherings frequently begin later than expected. However, professional and formal appointments require punctuality.

Dress Code:

Casual but tidy: Costa Ricans dress cleanly and conservatively. Casual clothes are allowed, but they must be clean and tidy. Avoid wearing beachwear outside of designated beach zones.

Respect Religious locations: When visiting churches or religious locations, wear modest clothing. Avoid wearing shorts, tank tops, and exposing apparel.

Dinner Etiquette:

Wait to Be Seated: In restaurants, customers must wait for the staff to seat them. If unsure, simply ask, "Puedo sentarme?" (Can I sit?).

Tip Modestly: Tipping is optional but appreciated. A 10% service charge is frequently included on the bill. If not, a 10% tip is standard.

Use Utensils: Use utensils to eat, even for items that are traditionally eaten by hand in other cultures. This is seen as courteous and considerate.

Environmental Respect:

Costa Ricans value their country's natural beauty and are committed to conservation. Leave No Trace principles include not littering, protecting wildlife, and keeping on authorized pathways.

Water Conservation: Water is a valuable resource in Costa Rica. Be aware of your water consumption, particularly in rural and dry locations.

Communication style:

Indirect Communication: Costa Ricans frequently employ indirect communication to prevent conflict and promote harmony. They may be polite and refrain from saying "no" directly. Pay attention to nonverbal signs and read between the lines.

Politeness and Formality: Being polite is highly praised. Use "usted" (the formal "you") to address someone you don't know well or in formal situations.

Money & Payment:

The official currency is the Costa Rican Colón (CRC), but US dollars are often accepted in tourist destinations. For smaller transactions, having some local cash comes in handy.

Credit cards are generally accepted, but it's always a good idea to keep cash on hand for markets, street sellers, and small businesses.

Respect for local customs:

Holy Week & Religious Festivals: Costa Rica is largely Catholic, and religious festivals like Semana Santa (Holy Week) are frequently celebrated. During certain occasions, some businesses may be closed, and there may be processions and festivities to attend.

Excessive public demonstrations of affection are uncommon, yet they are not discouraged. Simple hugs and kisses are acceptable.

Practical Travel Tips:

Health & Safety:

vaccines: Make sure you're up to date on routine vaccines. Determine whether any further immunizations or drugs are required for travel to Costa Rica.

Purchase comprehensive travel insurance that covers health issues, accidents, and travel delays.

Stay Hydrated and Sun-Protected: Tropical weather can be hot and humid. Drink lots of water, apply sunscreen, and wear a hat and sunglasses to protect yourself from the sun.

Transportation:

Buses are the most frequent mode of public transit, and they are generally reliable and economical. Taxis are also readily available. Make sure the cab is registered and the meter (maría) is used.

Car Rentals: If you want to explore rural locations, renting a car can be useful. Roads can be difficult, particularly in rural areas, thus a 4x4 vehicle is recommended.

Domestic Flights: For lengthy distances, look into domestic flights offered by local carriers like Sansa and Nature Air.

Internet & Communication:

SIM Cards and Wi-Fi: Local SIM cards are available for purchase, offering inexpensive mobile data. Wi-Fi is readily provided in hotels, cafés, and public spaces.

Language Apps: Use language translation apps to improve communication. Google Translate and other tools can assist bridge linguistic gaps.

Respecting Nature and Wildlife:

Responsible Tourism: Select eco-friendly accommodations and tour operators that value sustainability and conservation.

Wildlife Viewing: Keep a safe distance from wildlife and avoid feeding them. Use binoculars to get a better look, and respect their natural habitats.

Traveling to Costa Rica is a rewarding experience, with spectacular natural beauty, genuine hospitality, and a rich cultural legacy. Learning a few key Spanish phrases, as well as understanding local customs and etiquette, will help you improve your interactions and make your visit more fun and courteous. Whether you're visiting bustling markets, dining at local restaurants, or interacting with the welcoming Tico people, these ideas and information will help you make the most of your vacation while respecting the traditions and values of this unique country. Accept the Pura Vida lifestyle and savor every moment of your Costa Rica vacation.

Conclusion

Costa Rica is a great tourism destination, offering an unrivaled blend of natural beauty, cultural depth, and friendly hospitality. Whether you're looking for adventure, nature, or relaxation, this Central American jewel has something for everyone. Here, we conclude our full exploration with opinions on why Costa Rica is a must-see, recommendations for making the most of your trip and closing thoughts on the Pura Vida lifestyle.

Costa Rica's various landscapes beckon exploration and discovery, from the cloud forests of Monteverde to the volcanic vistas of Arenal, the pristine beaches of Guanacaste, and the lively animals of Corcovado. Each location provides its distinct attractions and experiences, resulting in a mosaic of remarkable adventures.

Costa Rica's conservation efforts have conserved its diverse wildlife, making it a popular destination for eco-tourists. The country's national parks and reserves safeguard a diverse range of ecosystems, including rainforests, cloud forests, wetlands, and marine areas. Visitors can engage in activities such as bird viewing, hiking, snorkeling, and wildlife photography, all while helping to preserve these valuable environments.

Costa Rica's culture combines indigenous origins, Spanish colonial influences, and Afro-Caribbean features. The country's festivals, traditional crafts, and gastronomic delights provide a thorough exploration of its dynamic and diverse cultural landscape. Engaging with local communities through homestays, workshops, and tours allows you to make genuine connections and learn about Tico culture.

Costa Rica offers world-class surfing, white-water rafting, zip-lining, and other adrenaline-fueled activities. Simultaneously, the country is a wellness haven, with yoga retreats, hot springs, and holistic health centers offering relaxation and renewal in breathtaking natural surroundings.

Practical Travel Tips:

To thoroughly immerse yourself in Costa Rican culture, consider the following practical travel tips:

Although English is often spoken in tourist destinations, learning basic Spanish words can improve relationships and demonstrate respect for local culture. Simple greetings, polite expressions, and frequent queries can go a long way toward developing rapport with residents.

Respect culture and the environment by adopting the Pura Vida philosophy, which promotes a positive and calm lifestyle. Show respect for Costa Rican customs and etiquette, including greetings, social conventions, and environmental practices. To reduce your environmental impact, support local artists and companies, stay in eco-friendly accommodations, and practice responsible tourism.

To ensure your health and safety, get up-to-date vaccinations and seek travel insurance for protection against accidents. Stay hydrated, use sunscreen, and exercise caution when handling food and water in isolated regions. Familiarise yourself with emergency numbers and medical services near your trip destinations.

Costa Rica's public transport system is reliable and cost-effective, with buses linking key destinations. Consider hiring a car for more remote or flexible travel, but keep in mind that road conditions can fluctuate. Domestic flights cover huge distances, making it a useful way to reach remote locations fast.

Final Thoughts: Living Pura Vida

Pura Vida, which means "pure life," is more than simply a word; it represents the Costa Rican way of life. This attitude is evident in the country's emphasis on health, community, and environmental stewardship. Embracing Pura Vida entails appreciating simple pleasures, being present at the moment, and cultivating a cheerful and thankful mindset.

As you travel across Costa Rica, take the time to slow down and enjoy each experience. Allow the spirit of Pura Vida to guide you as you admire the beauty of a scarlet macaw in flight, savor the flavors of a traditional casado, or relax in Arenal's hot springs.

Plan Your Return: One trip to Costa Rica is frequently insufficient to experience everything this rich and dynamic country has to offer. Each tour reveals fresh delights and develops your relationship with the landscapes and people. As you plan your return, think of seeing different places, doing new activities, and immersing yourself in Costa Rica's cultural richness.

For future vacations, consider exploring lesser-known areas like the Osa Peninsula, Central Valley cultural hotspots, or the laid-back Caribbean coast. To have a long-term impact, learn more about Costa Rican culture, attend local festivals, and assist with conservation programs.

Costa Rica's seasons provide unique experiences. The dry season (December to April) is ideal for beach activities and clear skies, but the green season (May to November) offers lush landscapes, fewer tourists, and excellent opportunities for animal viewing.

Costa Rica's attractiveness stems from its natural beauty, cultural diversity, and the warmth of its people. It's a place where you may explore, discover, and connect. Embracing the Pura Vida lifestyle will not only enhance your vacation experience but will also leave you with a piece of Costa Rica's soul long after you return home.

As you reflect on your adventures and plan future trips, keep in mind that Costa Rica is a location where each visit yields fresh discoveries and deeper connections. It is a land where nature and culture coexist peacefully, with limitless chances for discovery and progress. Embrace the adventure, appreciate the land and its people, and let Costa Rica's magic inspire you to embrace the Pura Vida lifestyle.

Appendix

Useful Apps

Google Maps: Essential for navigation and finding places of interest.

Duolingo: A fun way to learn and practice Spanish on the go.

Google Translate: Useful for translating phrases and text between Spanish and English.

WhatsApp: Widely used in Costa Rica for communication.

XE Currency: To easily convert currencies and keep track of exchange rates.

Booking.com: For finding and booking accommodations.

Uber: Available in major cities like San José for convenient transportation.

iNaturalist: Helps identify plants and animals you encounter.

Trailforks: Useful for finding hiking trails.

Costa Rica Guide: Offers offline maps and travel guides specific to Costa Rica.

Emergency Contacts

National Emergency Number: 911

Tourist Police: +506 2257 8485

Red Cross: +506 2221 5818

Fire Department: +506 2221 5267

US Embassy in San José: +506 2519 2000

UK Embassy in San José: +506 2258 2025

Canada Embassy in San José: +506 2242 4400

Hospital CIMA (San José): +506 2208 1000

Hospital Clínica Bíblica (San José): +506 2522 1000

Useful Phrases

Hola: Hello

Buenos días: Good morning

Buenas tardes: Good afternoon

Buenas noches: Good evening/night

Adiós: Goodbye

Por favor: Please

Gracias: Thank you

De nada: You're welcome

Perdón: Excuse me/Sorry

Cuánto cuesta? How much does it cost?

Dónde está...? Where is...?

Habla inglés? Do you speak English?

Necesito ayuda: I need help

Dónde está el baño? Where is the bathroom?

La cuenta, por favor: The check, please

FAQs

1. Do I need a visa to travel to Costa Rica?

- Citizens from many countries, including the US, Canada, and the EU, do not need a visa for stays up to 90 days. Check the latest requirements based on your nationality.

2. What currency is used in Costa Rica?

    - The official currency is the Costa Rican Colón (CRC). US dollars are widely accepted, but it's useful to have local currency for small purchases.

3. Is it safe to drink tap water?

    - Tap water is generally safe to drink in most parts of Costa Rica, especially in major cities and tourist areas. In remote areas, it's advisable to use bottled water.

4. What is the best time to visit Costa Rica?

    - The dry season (December to April) is the most popular time to visit for sunny weather, but the green season (May to November) offers lush landscapes and fewer tourists.

5. What should I do in case of a medical emergency?

- Call 911 for emergencies. Major cities have excellent hospitals like CIMA and Clínica Bíblica. Ensure you have travel insurance that covers medical emergencies.

Travel Checklist

Documents:

- Passport (valid for at least 6 months)
- Visa (if required)
- Travel insurance
- Copies of important documents (passport, insurance, itinerary)
- Vaccination records

Money:

- Cash (local currency and USD)
- Credit/debit cards
- Travel wallet

Clothing:

- Lightweight clothing

- Rain jacket or poncho
- Swimwear
- Comfortable walking shoes
- Sandals
- Hat and sunglasses

Toiletries:

- Sunscreen
- Insect repellent
- Personal hygiene products
- Medications (if needed)

Technology:

- Smartphone and charger
- Power bank
- Camera
- Travel adapter

Miscellaneous:

- Reusable water bottle
- Travel guidebook or map
- Small backpack or daypack

- Snacks

Travel Itineraries

3-Day Itinerary

Day 1: San José

Morning: Arrive in San José, check into your hotel.

Afternoon: Visit the National Theatre and Gold Museum.

Evening: Dinner at a local restaurant and explore the nightlife.

Day 2: Arenal Volcano

Morning: Travel to Arenal Volcano (3-hour drive from San José).

Afternoon: Explore Arenal Volcano National Park.

Evening: Relax in the hot springs.

Day 3: Monteverde Cloud Forest

Morning: Travel to Monteverde (3-hour drive from Arenal).

Afternoon: Visit the Monteverde Cloud Forest Reserve.

Evening: Night walk tour to see nocturnal wildlife.

5-Day Itinerary

Day 1: San José

Morning: Arrive in San José, check into your hotel.

Afternoon: Visit the National Theatre and Central Market.

Evening: Dinner at a local restaurant.

Day 2: Tortuguero National Park

Morning: Travel to Tortuguero (4-5 hours, including boat transfer).

Afternoon: Explore Tortuguero Village and beach.

Evening: Night tour to see nesting turtles (seasonal).

Day 3: Arenal Volcano

Morning: Travel to Arenal Volcano.

Afternoon: Hike in Arenal Volcano National Park.

Evening: Relax in the hot springs.

Day 4: Monteverde Cloud Forest

Morning: Travel to Monteverde.

Afternoon: Visit the Monteverde Cloud Forest Reserve.

Evening: Night walk tour to see nocturnal wildlife.

Day 5: Return to San José

Morning: Canopy tour or hanging bridges in Monteverde.

Afternoon: Return to San José.

Evening: Farewell dinner.

7-Day Itinerary

Day 1: San José

Morning: Arrive in San José, check into your hotel.

Afternoon: Visit the National Theatre and Central Market.

Evening: Dinner at a local restaurant.

Day 2: Tortuguero National Park

Morning: Travel to Tortuguero.

Afternoon: Explore Tortuguero Village and beach.

Evening: Night tour to see nesting turtles (seasonal).

Day 3: Tortuguero National Park

Morning: Boat tour of the canals.

Afternoon: Visit the Tortuguero National Park.

Evening: Relax at your lodge.

Day 4: Arenal Volcano

Morning: Travel to Arenal Volcano.

Afternoon: Hike in Arenal Volcano National Park.

Evening: Relax in the hot springs.

Day 5: Monteverde Cloud Forest

Morning: Travel to Monteverde.

Afternoon: Visit the Monteverde Cloud Forest Reserve.

Evening: Night walk tour to see nocturnal wildlife.

Day 6: Monteverde and Santa Elena

Morning: Canopy tour or hanging bridges.

Afternoon: Visit the Santa Elena Cloud Forest Reserve.

Evening: Enjoy a local dinner.

Day 7: Return to San José

Morning: Travel back to San José.

Afternoon: Last-minute shopping or sightseeing.

Evening: Farewell dinner and prepare for departure.